Living Loved
Living Free

*Experience
the freedom
of living in the
Father's love,
through the
finished work
of Jesus*

by
CONNIE WITTER

because
of Jesus
publishing

Living Loved, Living Free

ISBN: 978-0-9779972-4-4
Copyright © 2010 by Because of Jesus Publishing

BECAUSE OF JESUS PUBLISHING
P.O. Box 3064
Broken Arrow, OK 74013

Cover design and layout: Nan Bishop, Tulsa, Oklahoma
nbishopsdesigns@cox.net
Edited by Rose Karlebach, Tulsa, Oklahoma
onlyroseofsharon@gmail.com

DEDICATION

This book is dedicated to my wonderful husband, Tony.
Thank you so much for loving and supporting me throughout the writing
of this book. I appreciate and love you more than you know.

ACKNOWLEDGEMENTS

To all my wonderful friends in Christ who have faithfully attended
the Bible Study and contributed to the writing of this book. I am
so very thankful for your friendship and support.

I especially want to thank the staff of
Because of Jesus Ministries:

Nancy Bishop, Art Director: your gift continues to amaze me;

Rose Karlebach, Editor: you are gifted in so many ways;

Lisa Aldrich, Office Administrator and Web Design:
I can't thank you enough for all you do;

Wayne and Marsha Rivers, Audio/Video Directors: you have both
been stuch an encouragement and blessing to me;

and Sherry Hensley, Marketing: thank you for reading through
the manuscript, and helping to spread the message of the
Good News we have in Jesus.

Your encouragement and suggestions are valuable to me;
I love and appreciate you all very much!

LIVING LOVED, LIVING FREE

EPHESIANS 1:1-14 PERSONALIZED FROM THE MESSAGE BIBLE

Heavenly Father, what a blessing You are! You take me to the high places of blessing in Jesus. Long before You laid down earth's foundations, You had me in mind, had settled on me as the focus of Your love, to be made whole and holy by Your love. Long, long ago You decided to adopt me into Your family through Jesus Christ. (What pleasure You took in planning this!) You wanted me to enter into the celebration of Your lavish gift-giving by the hand of Your beloved Son. Because of the sacrifice of Jesus, His blood poured out on the altar of the Cross, I have been set free — free of the penalties and punishments chalked up by my misdeeds. And not just barely free, either. Abundantly free! You thought of everything, provided for everything I could possibly need, letting me in on the plans You took such delight in making. You set it all out before me in Jesus, a long-range plan in which everything would be brought together and summed up in Him.

For it's in You, Jesus, that I find out who I am and what I am living for. Long before I first heard of You and got my hopes up, You had Your eye on me, had designs on me for glorious living, part of the overall purpose You are working out in everything and everyone.

And it's in You, Jesus, that I, once I heard the truth and believed it, found myself home free — signed, sealed, and delivered by the Holy Spirit. This signet from You is the first installment on what's coming, a reminder that I'll receive everything You have planned for me, a praising and glorious life.

EPHESIANS 3:17-21 PERSONALIZED FROM THE NEW LIVING TRANSLATION AND AMPLIFIED BIBLE

[17]Jesus, make Your home in my heart as I believe and trust You. May my roots grow down deep into Your marvelous love and keep me strong. [18]May I have the power to understand, as all God's people should, how wide, how long, how high, and how deep Your love is for me. [19]May I experience Your love, Jesus, though it is too great to fully understand. Then I will be made complete with all the fullness of life and power that comes from You. [20]Now, according to Your power that is at work within me, You are able to carry out Your purpose for my life and do superabundantly, far over and above all that I dare ask or think — infinitely beyond my highest prayers, desires, thoughts, hopes, or dreams!

TABLE OF CONTENTS

A Personal Note from the Author

Living Loved, Living Free was written from my own personal experience of learning to live in the Father's love. For many years of my Christian life I was held captive by the devil's lies which I know you've heard, too: "You're not good enough. They're better than you. Something is wrong with you. You lack in some way." I believed lies about myself, and God, and they kept me in bondage to fear, worry, condemnation, shame, and insecurity. Even though I was a daughter of the King, I lived like a fearful slave, trying to earn my Heavenly Father's blessing and approval instead of receiving it as a free gift of His grace. All of my effort was spent trying to be like Jesus, instead of embracing the truth that because of His gift of righteousness, I was already just like Him. I saw myself as lacking, instead of complete in Jesus. Because I really didn't know my Heavenly Father's amazing, unconditional, unchanging love, I wasn't enjoying the freedom that Jesus had purchased for me.

Within these pages is the truth the Holy Spirit revealed to me that has totally transformed my heart and my life. Each time I've read through this manuscript, I was once again overwhelmed with the Good News of the Father's love and grace toward me that has set my heart free. As I've learned to live in my Father's love, my heart has continually overflowed with love, joy, and the peace that passes all understanding. I now know how much He loves me and have put my trust in His love. I am living loved and living free!

I invite you to take this journey with me, and experience the freedom of living in the Father's love, through the finished work of Jesus. In our study of Ephesians Chapters 1-3, you'll realize that it is only in Jesus that you find out *who you really are* and *what you are living for*. You'll come to know for yourself a love so great that it satisfies every desire and need of your heart. This Bible study was written to help you identify and expose the lies the devil has used to keep you captive, and encourage you to live in the Father's love, where true freedom abounds. You'll discover the one lie the enemy tempts God's children to believe, and the one truth that has the power to set you completely free!

Jesus made it possible for us to live in the truth of the Father's love, but for far too long we have believed our enemy's lies. While the symptoms are clear: discouragement, depression, worry, fear, resentment, frustration, anger, insecurity, condemnation and pride, it's time for freedom. It's time to begin agreeing with the One Who loves you. As you discover who you truly are in Jesus, and come to believe it, you'll begin to live the glorious life He has always planned. You'll find true freedom in living loved by Him, and experience the abundant life that is your inheritance as a beloved child of the King. It is my prayer that you'll fill your heart with the truth, and you'll truly learn to live loved and live free!

Connie Witter

STUDY SUGGESTIONS

1. To make the most of your group study experience, we suggest you purchase the *Living Loved, Living Free DVDs* and the downloadable *Leader's Guide* from the Because of Jesus website at becauseofJesus.com. A complete Bible Study Package is also available on our website for groups of ten (10) or more participants.

2. If you do have more than ten (10) participants in your group study, we suggest you have several discussion leaders, one for each group, with a maximum of ten (10) people per discussion group. Keep in mind that the smaller the discussion group, the more comfortable each person will be in participating, and in sharing from their heart. You can print off multiple copies of the Leader's Guide so that each group discussion leader has a copy.

3. Hand out the workbooks a week before the study begins so that each participant has an opportunity to get his or her lessons done before the first week's meeting. In this way, the DVDs will be a review of the lesson they have already done.

4. Pray before you put in the DVD. Ask the Lord to open your eyes to the truth, and acknowledge Him as your true teacher.

5. Each DVD lesson will take approximately 45 minutes to view. Encourage the participants to take notes while they are listening so they can share what the Lord has shown them during group discussion. You will learn so much from listening to one another and from hearing yourself say what the Lord has taught you. What you share not only encourages others, but helps solidify the truth in your own heart.

6. Once the DVD is finished, have the participants break up into discussion groups of ten (10) or less participants.

7. Begin group discussions by asking each person what the Holy Spirit specifically spoke to him or her through the DVD teaching that week.

8. Choose a few questions from each day's study to discuss in your group.

9. Ask for any prayer requests and end your study with a word of prayer.

10. At the end of each group discussion, encourage participants to spend time with the Lord and in His word over the next week and remind them of which lesson they'll be studying the following week.

WEEK 1

Created to be Loved

DAY 1:
Created to be Loved

DAY 2:
Living Loved

DAY 3:
Ask, Listen, Respond

This week we'll begin our study in Ephesians 1:1-4:

¹This letter is from Paul, chosen by the will of God to be an apostle of Christ Jesus. I am writing to God's holy people in Ephesus, who are faithful followers of Christ Jesus. ²May God our Father and the Lord Jesus Christ give you grace and peace. ³All praise to God, the Father of our Lord Jesus Christ, who has blessed us with every spiritual blessing in the heavenly realms because we are united with Christ. ⁴Even before he made the world, God loved us and chose us in Christ to be holy and without fault in his eyes. NLT²

CREATED TO BE LOVED

Long before he laid down earth's foundations, he had us in mind, had settled on us as the focus of his love, to be made whole and holy by his love.

EPHESIANS 1:4 MSG

❧ *Take time to pray before you begin.* ❧

Let's begin by making Ephesians 1:3 and 4 personal. Write your name on the lines below:

³The Father has blessed _____ with every spiritual blessing in the heavenly realm because _____ is united with Jesus.

⁴Long before he laid down earth's foundations, he had _____ in mind, had settled on _____ as the focus of his love, to be made whole and holy by His love.

Before God created the world, you were on His mind. He wanted sons and daughters that He could love. He settled on you as the focus of His love. Through making you one with Jesus, God planned to make your heart whole by His love.

Whole means "to be complete; to lack nothing." It has always been God's plan for you to feel complete; for your heart to be whole; for you to lack nothing. He created you to find your identity and worth in His love for you. His plan was to fill every need in your heart with His love so that you were completely satisfied and fulfilled in your relationship with Him. 1 John 4:8 says, *God is love.* You were created to be loved by Him.

If God is love and He created us to be made whole by His love, then why is the world in such a mess? Didn't God, in His love for us, promise us peace, love, and overflowing joy? Then why are there so many hurting people with broken hearts? And why do so many of God's people seem to be wandering in a wilderness of shame, confusion, fear, insecurity, depression and disappointment?

LET'S TAKE A LOOK INTO THE WORD OF GOD TO FIND THE ANSWER.

In the beginning, God created man and woman. He loved them and His opinion of them was very good.

Read **Genesis 1:26, 27, 31:** *²⁶Then God said, "Let us make people in our image to be like ourselves." ²⁷So God created people in His own image… ³¹Then God looked over all he had made, and he saw that it was excellent in every way. NLT¹*

*³¹And God saw everything that He had made, and behold, **it was very good**… and He **approved it completely**. AMP*

*31 God looked over everything he had made; **it was so good, so very good!*** MSG

What was God's opinion of Adam and Eve? How did He feel about them? Look at verse 31 in each translation.

_____

_____

_____

God looked at Adam and Eve and saw Himself. He had created them in His image. They were just like Him. As He lovingly admired His son and daughter He said, *You are excellent in every way! You are so good, so very good! I approve of you completely!* He had a very good opinion of them. Adam and Eve were God's dream. He had created them to be the focus of His love.

Read **Genesis 2:25:** *Now, although Adam and his wife were both naked, neither of them felt any shame.* NLT¹

What were their hearts free from? What do you think their hearts were full of?

_____

_____

Their hearts were free from shame. They were free from any negative opinion of themselves or each other. They were free from any sense of lack. They received God's love into their hearts and believed His good opinion of them. They had His approval, His acceptance, and it made them feel valuable and loved by Him. Every need of their heart was met and they lacked nothing. They felt complete in His love.

THEN SOMETHING HAPPENED THAT CHANGED THE WAY ADAM AND EVE FELT ABOUT THEMSELVES.

Read **Genesis 3:1-6:** *¹Now the serpent was the shrewdest of all the creatures the LORD God had made. "Really?" he asked the woman, "Did God really say you must not eat any of the fruit in the garden?" ²"Of course we may eat it," the woman told him. ³"It's only the fruit from the tree at the center of the garden that we are not allowed to eat. God says we must not eat it or even touch it, or we will die." ⁴"You won't die!" the serpent hissed. ⁵"God knows that your eyes will be opened when you eat it. You will become just like God, knowing everything, both good and evil."*

⁶The woman was convinced. The fruit looked so fresh and delicious, and it would make her so wise! So she ate some of the fruit. She also gave some to her husband, who was with her. Then he ate it, too. NLT¹

The devil wanted to separate Adam and Eve from their love relationship with God, so he deceived them into believing three (3) lies:

15

1. You can't trust what God says. What He says about you isn't true. (Verse 1)
2. You're not like God. You lack in some way. (Verse 5)
3. You need to *do something* to be like God. You need to fix yourself and your spouse. (Verses 5 and 6)

- The truth is that God loved Adam and Eve completely. They could trust Him because everything God says is true (Proverbs 30:5).
- The truth is that they were made in God's image. They were already like God. They were complete in Him. They lacked nothing. (Genesis 1:26)
- The truth is Eve *didn't need to do anything* to fix herself or her husband because they were already excellent in every way. They were very good just as God had said. (Genesis 1:31)

Eve chose to believe the lies of the enemy. She doubted what God said about her and felt lack in her heart, so she looked outside of her relationship with God to make her heart feel complete. She tried to fix herself and Adam by eating from the tree of the knowledge of good and evil, and what was the end result?

Read **Genesis 3:7**: *At that moment, their eyes were opened, and they suddenly felt shame at their nakedness. NLT[1]*

Shame means:

- A painful emotion caused by consciousness of guilt or failure
- Judging yourself unworthy; unlovable; a negative opinion about yourself
- The state of having lost the respect (or good opinion) of others

Shame entered into their hearts, which had once been whole and complete, and filled with God's love. They immediately began to judge themselves and each other as bad, unworthy, and unlovable, so they hid from God. Because they exchanged God's good opinion of themselves for the enemy's lies, their hearts were broken.

As a result, sin and shame entered into the human race which caused the hearts of everyone God created to be broken (Romans 5:12). Ever since Adam and Eve, the enemy has deceived all of us into believing the same three lies. And just like Eve, we've all gone outside of our relationship with God to get the needs of our hearts met, leaving us brokenhearted.

A *broken heart* is one that lacks peace, confidence, security, and joy. To be brokenhearted means "to be disheartened by circumstances; discouraged, depressed, defeated, or disappointed."

- Have you ever experienced a broken heart by believing the enemy's lies?
- Have you ever looked at your failures and felt shame in your heart?

- Have you ever judged yourself unworthy, unlovable, or had a negative opinion of yourself?
- Have you ever felt like you lost the good opinion of your Heavenly Father?

AT ONE TIME OR ANOTHER, WE'VE ALL FALLEN FOR THE DEVIL'S LIES AND HAVE ENDED UP FEELING SHAME IN OUR HEARTS.

Although shame may have created brokenness within your heart, your Heavenly Father had a plan before the foundation of the world, to redeem you and heal your heart with His love. In **Genesis 3:15,** God spoke to the serpent and said, *"From now on, you and the woman will be enemies, and your offspring and her offspring will be enemies. He will crush your head, and you will strike his heel." NLT[1]*

God prophesied of a Redeemer who would come from the womb of a woman and would crush the enemy's head. His name is Jesus. **1 John 3:8** says, *"...the devil has sinned...from the beginning. The reason the Son of God was made manifest ...was to undo (destroy, loosen, dissolve) the works [of] the devil." AMP*

The *works of the devil* is sin which creates shame in the hearts of God's children. Jesus destroyed the works of the devil by becoming the sacrifice needed to take away our sin and shame in order to make our hearts whole once again.

Jesus reconciled you back to the Father's good opinion so that you would never again have to live in shame. No matter what mistakes you and I may have made in our past; no matter what mistakes we may make today or in our future, our Heavenly Father's good opinion of us will never change, because He looks at us through the blood of Jesus.

Read **Ephesians 1:3-4:** *[3]All praise to God, the Father of our Lord Jesus Christ, who has blessed us with every spiritual blessing in the heavenly realms because we are united with Christ. [4]Even before he made the world, God loved us and chose us in Christ **to be holy and without fault in his eyes.** NLT[2]*

Read **2 Corinthians 5:21:** *Christ did no wrong thing. But for our sake God put the blame for our wrong ways on Christ. So now **God sees us as good,** because we are in Christ. WE*

What is your Heavenly Father's good opinion of you because of Jesus? According to the two previous verses, what does He see when He looks at you in Christ?

_____

_____

God created you to be loved by Him. He created you with the need in your heart for unconditional love that only He could fill. He knew you would fail by believing the lies of the enemy just like Adam and Eve. He knew your heart would feel

shame and become broken, and before you were even born, He had a plan in place to redeem you through Jesus. His plan was to restore you back into His favor by cleansing you from all your sin through the blood of Jesus.

In the very same way He looked at Adam and Eve in the beginning, your Heavenly Father looks at you through the blood of Jesus and says: (write your name on the line below)

My Beloved _____,

You are excellent in every way! You are good, so very good, and I approve of you completely! You are without fault in my eyes because of your faith in my Son, Jesus, and there is nothing you could ever do to change My good opinion of you!

Your Heavenly Father

How does it make your heart feel to know that this is the way your Heavenly Father feels toward you?

_____

_____

Every day of your life the devil will tempt you with the same three lies he used on Eve. All three lies can be summed up in this one lie: **You're not who God says you are.** The devil knows that if you believe him, you'll go outside of your relationship with Jesus to meet the needs of your heart, and your heart will be filled with shame and brokenness.

In **Isaiah 61:1** and 2 Jesus said, "*…the LORD has anointed me to preach good news to the poor. He has sent me to bind up the brokenhearted, to proclaim freedom for the captives and release from darkness for the prisoners, ²to proclaim the year of the Lord's favor….*" *NIV*

Jesus came to make your heart whole with the Good News of God's love and acceptance. When you believe who you are in Christ, your heart is made whole and complete by His amazing love.

What is the main truth the Holy Spirit revealed to you in today's study and how will you apply it to your life?

_____

_____

_____

_____

Day 2

LIVING LOVED

*Long before he laid down earth's foundations, he had us in mind, had settled on us
as the focus of his love, to be made whole and holy by his love.*
EPHESIANS 1: 4 MSG

Take time to pray before you begin.

God created you with a deep need within your heart to be completely and
unconditionally loved. The Greek word for God's love in Ephesians 1:4 is *agape*.
(Strong's [26]) Agape love places value on the person being loved regardless of their
behavior. Unlike the kind of love the world offers, which is conditional and based
on your performance, agape (God's love) is an unconditional love that is not earned
based on what you do, how you behave, or how you look. It is given freely by God
based on who you are — the object of His affection.

Read **Romans 5:8-9**: *⁸But God showed his great love for us by sending Christ to
die for us while we were still sinners. NLT ²*

*⁹We are now justified (acquitted, made righteous, and brought into right relationship
with God) by Christ's blood. AMP*

What did you do to earn God's love? How did God prove He loves you
unconditionally? (Verse 8)

_____

_____

Because of God's great love for you, He didn't leave you as a sinner. What is your
new identity in Jesus? (Verse 9)

_____

_____

You did nothing to earn or deserve God's love. God proved His unconditional
love for you by sending Jesus to die for you when you were still a sinner. He loves you
so much that He didn't leave you in your sin. When you put your faith in Jesus, He
completely redeemed you by giving you a brand new identity. He didn't want you to
identify yourself with your sin and failure so He changed your identity completely.
He made you righteous in Christ. He wants your heart to be filled everyday with
this truth of His great love for you!

Ephesians 3:17-19 says, *¹⁷Then Christ will make his home in your hearts as you*

*trust in him. Your roots will grow down into God's love and keep you strong. ¹⁸And may you have the power to understand, as all God's people should, how wide, how long, how high, and how deep his love is. ¹⁹May you experience the love of Christ.... Then you will be made complete with all the **fullness** of life and power that comes from God.* NLT²

Your heart is God's dwelling place. He created your heart with the need to be filled up with complete approval, complete acceptance, and to feel completely valued. God is love and He is the only One who can truly meet every need of your heart and make your heart whole. Ephesians 3:17-19 teaches us that when we live in Christ's love we will truly feel complete and be filled with the fullness of life and power that comes from God.

The word *fullness* in this verse comes from the Greek word *pleroma*. It means "to fill up to completion." **Romans 5:5** says, *God's love has been poured out in our hearts through the Holy Spirit.* AMP God's love fills us up completely.

Colossians 2:9-10 says: *⁹For in Christ lives all the fullness of God in a human body. ¹⁰So you also are complete through your union with Christ....* NLT²

> *The fullness of God dwells in you because you are in Christ, and He is in you.*

The fullness of God dwells in you because you are in Christ, and He is in you. You are just like Him. You are complete and you lack nothing in Him. You are completely loved, completely righteous, completely accepted, completely approved, completely capable, and a complete success in Him. It is this Good News that Jesus was sent to tell you (Isaiah 61:1-11).

And yet, the devil is constantly trying to tempt you to look outside of Christ for your identity and worth. All of our hearts have been broken at one time or another because just like Adam and Eve, we have believed the lies of the enemy, and looked outside of Jesus to meet our need to be completely loved. Yesterday you learned that the three lies the devil tempted Eve with can be summed up in this one lie:

You're not who God says you are.

1. You can't trust what God says = *you're not who God says you are*

2. You lack in some way = *you're not who God says you are*

3. You need to do something to fix yourself = *you're not who God says you are*

If you believe any of the devil's lies, He has convinced you that *you're not who God says you are.*

FOR EXAMPLE:

LIES:	The Root of Every Lie	TRUTH:
You're not loved	= you're not who God says you are	John 15:9 Jesus says He loves you
You can't do it	= you're not who God says you are	Philippians 4:13 says you can do all things through Jesus
You're inadequate	= you're not who God says you are	Hebrews 13:21 says God has equipped you with everything you need to be a success
What if you fail?	= you're not who God says you are	Proverbs 16:3 says you are a success
You're not worthy	= you're not who God says you are	Col. 1:12-14 says Jesus has qualified you
They don't like you	= you're not who God says you are	Psalm 5:12 says God surrounds you with favor
You need to be productive to be valuable	= you're not who God says you are	1 Peter 1:18-19 says Jesus proved your value by paying for you with His blood
God isn't going to meet your needs	= you're not who God says you are	2 Corinthians 9:8 says all grace abounds toward you and God will abundantly supply your needs
You're not good enough	= you're not who God says you are	2 Corinthians 5:21 says you are the righteousness of God in Christ

The devil schemes every day in order to tempt you to believe this one lie. It may come in many different ways and through many different channels, but the root of every lie is always the same. If you believe that *you're not who God says you are*, then just like Adam and Eve, you'll look outside of your relationship with God to meet your sense of lack. It will bring shame and brokenness into your heart, and it will affect your life in a negative way. This one lie of the devil is intended to keep you from experiencing the fullness of life that is found in the love of Jesus.

Read **Romans 8:39**: *No power in the sky above or in the earth below—indeed, nothing in all creation will ever be able to separate us from the love of God that is revealed in Christ Jesus our Lord.* NLT [2]

Where can you find a revelation of God's love? Where is His love revealed?

A REVELATION OF GOD'S LOVE FOR YOU IS REVEALED IN WHO YOU ARE IN CHRIST.

Ephesians 1:11-14 says: *It's in Christ that we find out who we are and what we are living for. Long before we first heard of Christ and got our hopes up, he had his eye on us, had designs on us for glorious living, part of the overall purpose he is working out in everything and everyone. It's in Christ that you, once you heard the truth and believed it (this Message of your salvation), found yourselves home free — signed, sealed, and delivered by the Holy Spirit. This signet from God is the first installment on what's coming, a reminder that we'll get everything God has planned for us, a praising and glorious life.* MSG

It is in Christ that you find out who you are and what you are a living for. That is why the enemy is constantly tempting you to believe that you're not who God says you are. He knows if you ever discover who you really are in Christ and believe it, you'll truly live the glorious life that God has planned for you. You'll find true freedom in living loved by Him.

TWO WAYS TO LIVE

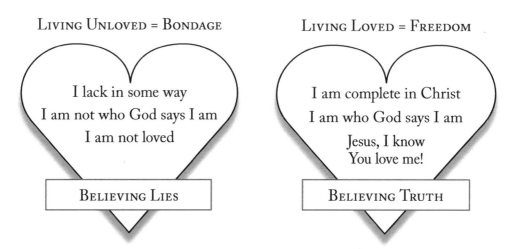

WHEN YOU BELIEVE YOUR HEAVENLY FATHER AND HIS OPINION OF YOU IN CHRIST, YOU ARE LIVING LOVED BY HIM.

I have come to realize that whenever my heart becomes sad or discouraged, the devil is tempting me to believe his lie: *I am not who God says I am.* Negative emotions indicate that I am feeling lack in my heart and am looking somewhere else besides Jesus to be completely loved.

Recently, my heart felt sad concerning my relationships with my two grown sons. For most of their lives, my sons have needed me on a pretty regular basis. Now that they are adults and living on their own, they don't need me as much as they used to. Because I hadn't heard from them in over a week, my heart began feeling sad as I thought, *Well, I guess they don't need me anymore.* As I recognized this sense of lack, I turned my thoughts to the Lord and said, "Lord, I'm feeling really sad. I feel like my boys don't need me anymore. Show me the truth that will set my heart free."

As I looked toward the Lord, His words of love began to flood my soul. I heard Him say, "Connie, you are looking to your boys to meet the need in your heart to feel valuable. I proved your value by paying for you with My blood. You don't need anybody else in this world to fill that need in your heart, but Me."

I realized then that I had been looking to my boys to determine my worth. Their need for me meant that I was valuable and it gave me a purpose in the world. But as I sat in the presence of the Lord, letting Him fill my heart with His love, the lie of the enemy was exposed and the truth of who I am in Jesus became very real to me. I responded, "Lord, I know You love me because You proved my value by laying Your life down for me. Thank You Lord, for filling that need in my heart and making me whole. My purpose for being here is to be loved by You and to love others with Your love."

The emotions you experience in your heart are an indicator of what you are believing. Be conscious of how your heart feels; realize that if you're experiencing negative emotions, the devil is tempting you to believe that you're not who God says you are. Turn to Jesus and ask Him to reveal the truth of who you are in Him. Let Him fill your heart with His great love. There is nothing else in the world that can completely satisfy your soul. You are complete in Jesus; created to be made whole, living loved by Him.

What one lie is the devil constantly tempting you to believe?

_____

_____

Look at the heart illustration again. What is the difference between living loved and living unloved?

_____

_____

How does it affect your life when you live loved?

_____

_____

_____

⚜ Day 3 ⚜
ASK, LISTEN, RESPOND

16 May He grant you out of the rich treasury of His glory to be strengthened and reinforced with mighty power in the inner man by the [Holy] Spirit...17 May Christ through your faith [actually] dwell...in your hearts! May you be rooted deep in love and founded securely on love, 18 That you may have the power and be strong to apprehend and grasp with all saints [God's devoted people, the experience of that love] what is the breadth and length and height and depth [of it]; 19 [That you may really come] to know [practically, through experience for yourselves] the love of Christ, which far surpasses mere knowledge... that you may be filled [through all your being] unto all the fullness of God.... 20 Now to Him Who, by... the [action of His] power that is at work in us, is able to [carry out His purpose and] do superabundantly, far over and above all that we [dare] ask or think [infinitely beyond our highest prayers, desires, thoughts, hopes, or dreams] — 21 To Him be glory in the church and in Christ Jesus throughout all generations forever and ever! Amen.

EPHESIANS 3:16-21 AMP

⚜ *Take time to pray before you begin.* ⚜

What is God able to do in your life as you become secure in the love of Christ and learn to live loved by Him? (Verse 20)

_____

_____

_____

WHAT A POWERFUL PASSAGE OF SCRIPTURE!

These verses have shown me that everything my heart desires is found in knowing the love that Jesus has for me. The fullness of God and His life and power working in my heart and life has everything to do with me learning to live in His love. As you and I abide in His love, He is able to bring to pass His purpose for our lives and do superabundantly, far over and above our highest prayers, desire, thoughts, hopes and dreams.

Read **1 Corinthians 14:1:** *Go after a life of love as if your life depended on it — because it does.* MSG

***Eagerly pursue** and seek to acquire [this] love [make it your aim, your great quest].* AMP

The word *love* in this verse is *agape*. It is the unconditional, unfailing love of Jesus. According to this verse, what does your very life depend on? What should be your great quest in life?

_____

_____

This verse made it very clear to me that my very life depends on me knowing and believing the love that God has for me. This love is found in Christ, and understanding this love has become my life's passion and my great quest. I want to think, act and love like Jesus. I want His life and power working in me. I want to experience the fullness of life that is found in living loved by Him. Because of this great desire, I asked the Lord, "How do I gain a deeper revelation of Your love? How do I learn to live loved by You?"

In response to my question, I heard the Lord say, *"Ask, listen, and respond,"* and then He showed me this truth very clearly in His Word. I realized that this is how all revelation from God comes into a person's heart.

ASK

Inspired by the Holy Spirit, the Apostle Paul prayed in Ephesians 3:16, that you would be strengthened by the Holy Spirit to believe the love that Jesus has for you. The Holy Spirit is the One Who gives you revelation of who you are in Jesus and then empowers you to believe it.

Ephesians 1:16-18 says: *¹⁶I have not stopped giving thanks for you, remembering you in my prayers. ¹⁷ **I keep asking** that the God of our Lord Jesus Christ, the glorious Father, may give you the Spirit of wisdom and revelation, so that you may know him better. ¹⁸I pray also that the eyes of your heart may be enlightened in order that you may know the hope to which he has called you, the riches of his glorious inheritance in the saints.* NIV

Jesus said in **Luke 11:9,10,13:** *⁹So I say to you, **Ask and keep on asking** and it shall be given you; seek and keep on seeking and you shall find; knock and keep on knocking and the door shall be opened to you. ¹⁰**For everyone who asks and keeps on asking receives**; and he who seeks and keeps on seeking finds; and to him who knocks and keeps on knocking, the door shall be opened. ¹³ If you then, evil as you are, know how to give good gifts…to your children, how much more will your heavenly Father give the Holy Spirit **to those who ask and continue to ask Him!** AMP

James 4:2 says: *You do not have, because you do not **ask** God.* NIV

What do these verses tell you about the importance of asking God for a revelation of His love for you?

_____

_____

LISTEN

In **Proverbs 4:20-22** God says: *²⁰My child, pay attention to what I say.* **Listen carefully** *to my words.* *²¹Don't lose sight of them. Let them penetrate deep into your heart,* *²² for they bring life to those who find them, and healing to their whole body.* NLT

What is your Heavenly Father admonishing you to do in Proverbs 4:20-21?

_____

_____

_____

If you listen to His words of love and let them penetrate deep into your heart, what will they bring to you? (Verse 22)

_____

_____

_____

RESPOND

In **Proverbs 22:17-19** God says: *¹⁷**Listen**…to the words of the wise, and apply your mind to my knowledge;* *¹⁸ For it will be pleasant if you keep them in your mind [believing them];* *your lips will be accustomed to [confessing] them.* *¹⁹ So that your trust (belief, reliance, support, and confidence) may be in the Lord.…* AMP

How did God say you can come to a place of complete trust in Him and His love for you?

Verse 17: _____

Verses 18 and 19:_____

ASK, LISTEN, RESPOND

When I read these verses in the Bible it helped me to understand how a revelation of God's love and the freedom He offers in Christ is available to everyone if they will simply **ask, listen** and **respond** to what Jesus has done for them.

ASK: For so long in my Christian life, I looked to others to teach me the truth, but what I didn't realize is that Jesus wanted me to look to Him. God does use pastors and teachers to share His Word with us, but He wants us looking to Him for revelation and understanding. The Holy Spirit is the One who leads us into all truth when we ask Him. My journey to freedom began with this simple prayer, "Lord, show me the truth that will set me free." I continue to ask every day for a deeper revelation of who I am in Christ and His great love for me. I know that true freedom is found in living loved by Him.

LISTEN: When I began to ask for a revelation of His love, I began to hear the Holy Spirit speak to me through God's word. The Scriptures opened up to me like never before. Instead of seeing a law that I needed to try to live up to, I began to see Jesus and who I am in Him. His love became very real to me as the Holy Spirit illuminated what Jesus really accomplished for me on the cross, and He gave me the power to believe it.

RESPOND: As I looked to Jesus, and received His love, I was empowered by the Holy Spirit to let go of the lies I had believed and to truly believe Jesus. I responded to His word by continually agreeing with Him. My lips became accustomed to saying the same thing I heard my Father say about me and my family. As I did this, my heart overflowed with thanksgiving and His words of love set my heart free.

As I have continued in this journey, I have become very aware that I need a daily revelation of who I am in Jesus and His great love for me. Yesterday's manna won't do. Every day the devil looks for an opportunity to tempt me to believe that I am not who God says I am. I must look to Jesus one more time for the revelation and strength to believe Him, instead.

The other day I became very frustrated while working on this manuscript because it just wasn't flowing. I had already spent hours working on it and I felt like I had accomplished nothing. I felt like God wasn't helping me; I had asked Him to help me, but He seemed so far away. So, I turned to Him and asked, "Lord, where are You? I asked You to help me, but You're not helping me." No sooner had I asked, when I recognized that I was believing a lie, because of the frustration I was feeling in my heart.

> *I asked, "Lord, show me the truth. Set my heart free."*

So, once again, **I asked**, "Lord, show me the truth. Set my heart free." Gently and sweetly, the Lord showed me that while I was waiting on Him to help me, He was waiting on me to agree with who I am in Jesus. He had already given me everything I needed to successfully write this manuscript.

Rather than continue to be frustrated, **I listened** as He spoke His words of love to me and reminded me, one more time, of who I am in Jesus. The Holy Spirit reminded me of Hebrews 13:21 which says *I am equipped through Christ with everything I need to carry out His will.* He also reminded me of Isaiah 61:1 and 1 John 2:20 which say *I am anointed in Christ to open up the eyes of the blind and set the captives free,* and Philippians 4:13 which says *I can do all things through Christ who strengthens me.*

Because of the Lord's encouraging words of love, **I responded** by saying, "Thank You, Jesus, for equipping me with everything I need to carry out Your will. I have Your wisdom, Your strength, and Your anointing to write this manuscript. I am qualified and anointed to set the captives free because You live in me." As I responded to His truth, I was empowered by the Holy Spirit to put my full confidence and

trust in Him. Shortly afterwards, I sat down and wrote the end of this very week, the words flowing out of me like rivers of living water.

Learning to live loved is a daily journey. Your very life depends on becoming established in the love of Jesus and understanding who you truly are in Him. Jesus longs for an intimate relationship with you. He is waiting for you to **ask, listen** and **respond**. So bring the cares and needs of your heart to Him, and ask Him to reveal the truth of His great love. Listen as He exposes the lies of the devil and enlightens your heart to who you truly are in Jesus. Then respond to Him with a heart of thanksgiving. You will be strengthened by the Holy Spirit to believe that you are truly loved and you'll experience the fullness of life that God has planned for you.

How can you receive a deeper understanding of God's love for you and learn to trust Him with all of your heart?

_____

_____

_____

_____

What is the main truth the Holy Spirit revealed to you in today's study?

_____

_____

_____

_____

_____

_____

_____

_____

_____

WEEK 2

The Fight for Your Heart

DAY 1:
The Fight for Your Heart

DAY 2:
Breaking Free from the Enemy's Lies

DAY 3:
Agree with the One Who Loves You

¹⁷May Christ through your faith [actually] dwell (settle down, abide, make His permanent home) in your hearts! May you be rooted deep in love and founded securely on love, ¹⁸That you may have the power and be strong to apprehend and grasp with all the saints [God's devoted people, the experience of that love] what is the breadth and length and height and depth [of it]; ¹⁹[That you may really come] to know [practically, through experience for yourselves] the love of Christ, which far surpasses mere knowledge [without experience]; that you may be filled [through all your being] unto all the fullness of God [may have the richest measure of the divine Presence, and become a body wholly filled and flooded with God Himself]! ²⁰Now to Him Who, by (in consequence of) the [action of His] power that is at work within us, is able to [carry out His purpose and] do superabundantly, far over and above all that we [dare] ask or think [infinitely beyond our highest prayers, desires, thoughts, hopes, or dreams] — ²¹To Him be glory in the church and in Christ Jesus throughout all generations forever and ever. Amen (so be it).

EPHESIANS 3:17-21 AMP

⌘ Day 1 ⌘
THE FIGHT FOR YOUR HEART

*¹⁷May Christ through your **faith** [actually] dwell (settle down, abide,*
*make His permanent home) in your **hearts**! May you be rooted deep in love*
and founded securely on love.

EPHESIANS 3:17 AMP

⌐ Take time to pray before you begin. ⌐

By the inspiration of the Holy Spirit, the Apostle Paul prayed that through your faith, Jesus would dwell and abide in your heart and you would become rooted deeply and securely in His love.

The word *heart* in Ephesians 3:17 comes from the Greek word *kardia (Strong's ²⁵⁸⁸)*. According to *Strong's Concordance* it means, "your thoughts, your feelings; your mind." The *Lexical Aids to the New Testament* defines it as "the very seat of your will."

Your heart is your mind, thoughts, and emotions. It is where you decide what you believe. Often the beliefs of your heart are established by what you've experienced in life, what you've been taught, or how you've been treated. The Apostle Paul was praying in Ephesians 3:17 that the beliefs of your heart would be centered in Christ and what He has accomplished for you. He prayed that your mind, your thoughts, and your emotions would be filled with the truth of who you are in Jesus and His great love for you.

YOUR HEART IS WHERE ALL YOUR BELIEFS ARE STORED

Romans 10:10 says: *For it is with your heart that you believe.... NIV*

What you truly believe about God, Jesus, prayer, your spouse, your children, success, finances, righteousness, etc., is stored in your heart. In every area of your life you either believe the truth of what God says or the lies of the devil. In the areas of your heart where you believe the devil's lies, they will bring forth shame, fear, and disappointment. In the areas of your heart where you believe the truth of what God says about you, they will bring forth His glory.

Look back at the heart diagram and let's use your weight as an example. If you believe the devil's lies and your heart belief is that *I can't control myself,* or *I'm a failure in this area,* or *I need food* (to meet an emotional need), then you'll struggle with weight all your life, feeling shame and disappointment with yourself. But if you truly believe down deep in your heart that what God says is true about you, such as *I have self-control. I am a healthy person. I don't need food,* (to meet an emotional need) *because I know He loves me,* then you'll experience the glory of God in this area of your life and you'll maintain a healthy weight.

Let's take a look at another area, finances, for example. If you believe the devil's lies and the belief of your heart is that you lack, you'll be reluctant to give and bless others, you'll be discontent, make poor financial decisions, and you'll never feel like you have enough. You'll experience shame, fear, and disappointment in this area of your life. But if you believe down deep in your heart that what God says about you is true (regardless of what you may be experiencing in your life right now) you will think, *I am abundantly blessed because of Jesus. Lord, Your grace abounds toward me and I have more than enough to meet my needs. I am a good steward of what You have given me.* Then you'll freely give, be content and happy, make wise financial decisions and live in the abundant blessings of God. You'll experience peace and glorify God is this area of your life.

WHAT YOU BELIEVE IN YOUR HEART IS WHAT YOU'LL EXPERIENCE IN YOUR LIFE

Proverbs 23:7 says: *As [a man] thinks in his heart, so is he. AMP*

What you believe about yourself down deep in your heart will manifest in your life.

I've been a Christian my entire life, but it was not until I was twenty four years old that I truly began to experience the fullness of life that Jesus died to give me. For most of my life, I felt lack in almost every area. I believed the devil's lies. My heart belief about myself was that I lacked and that is exactly what I experienced. I lacked confidence, peace, joy, love, finances, favor, friendships, security, satisfaction and fulfillment because the belief of my heart was determining the fruit of my life.

Proverbs 27:19 says: *As the water reflects the face, so the heart reflects the person. HCSB*

MY LIFE REFLECTED THE BELIEFS OF MY HEART.

The transformation in my life really started when I began to devote my heart, my mind and my thoughts to Jesus. I began to continually think on the truth of who I am in Him and talk to Him daily about what He said about me. My mind began to be filled with thoughts like this: *Jesus, I know You love me because You died to make me righteous in You. Thank You for surrounding me with favor as a shield. I know You love me, Lord, because You approve of me. I am abundantly blessed because of You.* God's word began to penetrate deep within my heart and my heart beliefs started changing to those of abundance. My sense of lack disappeared, and what God said about me began to manifest in my life. I began to experience an abundance of peace, joy, friendships, favor, finances, as I became secure in the love of Jesus. As you get your mind on Jesus, your heart becomes full of life. Any death in your soul dissipates in the light of Jesus and you feel alive and free. You are filled with the fullness of God.

God has an amazing plan for your life, but there is a fight going on for your heart. You are part of a royal race, chosen by God to receive His love and be like Him on the earth. **1 Peter 2:9** says this: *⁹But you are a chosen race, a royal priesthood, a dedicated nation, [God's] own purchased, special people, that you may set forth the wonderful deeds and display the virtues and perfections of Him Who called you out of darkness into His marvelous light. AMP*

Who are you according to this verse?

_____

As young children, we love royal adventure stories, where a princess is rescued by the handsome prince, or a young man overcomes evil, saves the princess, and becomes a king. These stories appeal to us because we are part of the royal family of God, and we want to take our rightful place in His kingdom.

It is interesting to note that in all of these stories there is always an evil person who lies to the prince or princess' heart in order to distract them from their royal destiny. You have an enemy too — the devil — who is constantly telling you that, *You're not complete; you lack in some way. You're not who God says you are.*

There are two fighting for your heart. Jesus, the One Who loves you, is waiting for you to turn toward Him and invite Him to fill your heart with His words of love. The enemy, however, doesn't need any invitation, he begins his plan to fill your heart with lies from the moment you are born.

Read **John 10:10:** *The thief comes only in order to steal and kill and destroy. I came that they may have and enjoy life and have it in abundance to the full, until it overflows. AMP*

What is the devil's plan for your heart and life?

_____

What is Jesus' plan for your heart and life?

There are clearly two plans for your life. Whom you choose to believe down deep in your heart will determine the course of your life.

> Read **Proverbs 4:20-23**: *²⁰My child, pay attention to what I say. Listen carefully to my words. ²¹Don't lose sight of them. Let them penetrate deep into your heart, ²²for they bring life to those who find them, and healing to their whole body. ²³Guard your heart above all else, for it determines the course of your life.* NLT²
>
> **Proverbs 4:23**: *²³Carefully guard your thoughts because they are the source of true life.* CEV

What does Jesus want your mind and heart to be full of? (Verses 20 and 21)

If you let His words penetrate deep into your heart, what will they bring to you? (Verse 22)

Look at verse 23 in both translations. Why is it important to guard your heart and mind above everything else you do?

In these verses your Heavenly Father admonishes you to pay attention to what He says. Listen carefully to the promises of His word. Don't be distracted by the devil's lies, or what anyone else has to say. Let His words penetrate deep within your heart. This is to think deeply about what He says and let His word become the center of who you are and the core of what you believe. True abundant life is experienced when the belief of your heart has nothing to do with what you feel, hear or see, but everything to do with who you are in Jesus and what God says is true about you. Circumstances are subject to change, but the truth remains the same.

When you believe God's words of love to be true, they will bring life and health to you. The word *life* in verse 22 comes from the Hebrew words *chay* and *chayah* which mean, "to give promise, to restore, and to make whole." (*Strong's ²⁴²¹*) The words that God speaks are alive and full of power (Hebrews 4:12). When you keep them in the center of your heart by keeping your thoughts on who you are in Christ, they will bring the manifestation of God's promises into every area of your life.

The word *health* in verse 22 comes from the Hebrew word *marpe (Strong's ⁴⁸³²)* which means "a medicine or a cure, deliverance, and healing." The word health is also derived from the Hebrew word *rapha* which is a word that describes God Himself, which means "to heal; a physician who thoroughly makes one whole." (*Strong's ⁷⁴⁹⁵*)

Whoever you choose to believe is whose plan will come to pass in your life.

This is why God said in verse 23 that above everything you do in life guard your heart. What you let into your thoughts and heart will become what you believe, and your heart beliefs will affect your life in a positive or negative way. Out of the beliefs of your heart will come the issues of your life. This is why you have two fighting for your heart. They each want you to devote your thoughts to their words and believe them down deep in your heart because whoever you choose to believe is whose plan will come to pass in your life. The devil's plan is to steal your joy and peace so that your heart is filled with shame, insecurity and fear. Jesus, on the other hand, came to fill your heart with His love so that you could enjoy life and have it in abundance, to the full, till it overflows with peace, joy, love, security and blessing!

Jesus is the One Who loves you.

He desperately wants you to bring your heart to Him and fill your mind and thoughts with His words of love. He wants you to guard your heart from the lies of the enemy and choose to believe Him instead. If you want to live in the fullness of life that Jesus came to give you, you must decide that you're done believing the lies of your enemy and turn to Jesus and say, "Jesus, My heart belongs to You. Show me the lies of the devil that I have believed and help me to believe what You say about me. Help me to live in Your love."

What is the main truth the Holy Spirit revealed to you in today's study and how will you apply it to your life?

⊰ Day 2 ⊱

BREAKING FREE FROM THE ENEMY'S LIES

*But now I am fearful, lest that even as the serpent beguiled Eve by his cunning,
so your minds may be corrupted and seduced from wholehearted
and sincere and pure devotion to Christ.*

2 CORINTHIANS 11:3 AMP

⊰ *Take time to pray before you begin.* ⊱

Inspired by the Holy Spirit, the Apostle Paul warned you in this scripture, of the devil's plan to deceive your heart with the same lies he used on Eve. Jesus has told you that you are very good and He approves of you completely! Yet, Paul feared that just as the serpent deceived Eve, he would also deceive you into believing that you're not who God says you are. He feared your mind would be corrupted and your heart would be turned away from your pure devotion to Jesus.

Read **John 8:44:** *[T]he Devil... was a murderer from the beginning and has always hated the truth. There is no truth in him. When he lies, it is consistent with his character, for he is a liar and the father of lies.* NLT²

What is the character of the devil?

_____

1 Peter 5:8-9 says: *⁸Stay alert! Watch out for your great enemy, the devil. He prowls around like a roaring lion, looking for someone to devour. ⁹Stand firm against him, and be strong in your faith.* NLT²

What do these verses encourage you to do and why?

_____

_____

Read **Ephesians 6:16:** *Above all, taking the shield of faith with which you will be able to quench all the fiery darts of the wicked one.* NKJV

How can you stop all the fiery darts aimed at your heart by Satan?

_____

_____

Those fiery darts are the lies of the devil intended to penetrate deep within your heart so that you will be in bondage to fear, insecurity and shame. The devil's only power is deception and if he can get you to agree with his lies, then you'll experience his plan for your life. **1 Peter 5:8-9** tells you to stay alert and be aware of your great enemy's plan to devour you with his lies. Resist him and stand firm in your faith.

THE SYMPTOMS OF THE DEVIL'S LIES ARE NEGATIVE EMOTIONS

In order to guard your heart from the lies of the enemy, you must first recognize when you're being tempted to believe a lie. Remember: **every lie the devil throws at you produces negative emotions**.

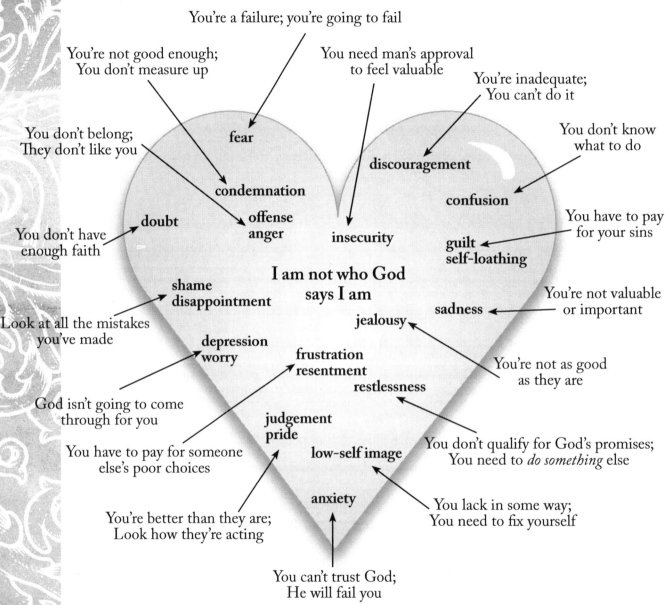

You're a failure; you're going to fail

You're not good enough; You don't measure up

You need man's approval to feel valuable

You're inadequate; You can't do it

You don't belong; They don't like you

You don't know what to do

fear

discouragement

confusion

condemnation

doubt

offense anger

insecurity

guilt self-loathing

You don't have enough faith

You have to pay for your sins

I am not who God says I am

shame disappointment

sadness

You're not valuable or important

Look at all the mistakes you've made

jealousy

depression worry

frustration resentment

You're not as good as they are

restlessness

God isn't going to come through for you

judgement pride

low-self image

You don't qualify for God's promises; You need to *do something* else

You have to pay for someone else's poor choices

anxiety

You're better than they are; Look how they're acting

You lack in some way; You need to fix yourself

You can't trust God; He will fail you

Have you ever heard these lies? Circle the ones the devil has tempted you to believe.

The Bible makes it very clear that anxiety, condemnation, sadness, worry, guilt, discouragement, depression, fear, offense, bitterness, contention, pride, confusion, unrest, insecurity, judgmental thoughts toward someone and anger are all symptoms of believing the lies of the devil. (See Ephesians 4:26-27; James 3:14-16; and 2 Timothy 2:25-26.)

When you agree with the lies of the enemy, his fiery darts penetrate your heart and create emotional wounds that bring disappointment and heartache into your life. These lies produce negative emotions. You can always know when you're being tempted to believe a lie by how it makes your heart feel. When you feel negative emotions in your heart, be aware that the enemy is tempting you to believe a lie and turn your heart and thoughts back to Jesus.

> *You can always know when you're being tempted to believe a lie by how it makes your heart feel.*

A RECENT EXAMPLE

My most recent experience with this occurred just the other day as I was writing this Bible Study. The devil came once again to try and tempt me to quit by throwing his lies at my heart. Just like the Apostle Paul warned me in 2 Corinthians 11:2-3, the devil was trying to corrupt my mind so that my heart would be turned away from my pure devotion to Jesus.

I began to feel sad and discouraged, and wasn't quite sure why, but the symptoms were loud and clear. It's at these moments that I have learned that if I want to live free, I must take my heart to Jesus and allow Him to shine the light of His truth on any darkness in my soul. So while I was driving to pick up my girls from school, I began talking to Jesus. "Lord, I'm feeling sad and discouraged about writing this study. Show me the lie that I'm believing and help me to believe You." I began to realize that the devil was tempting me to believe these lies: *It's too hard to write this Bible Study. It won't make a difference anyway, so why waste your time. It won't be any good or help anyone, so go do something else.*

So, I said, "Lord, I know this is not the truth, but it's how I feel at this moment, and honestly I feel like quitting. Strengthen me by Your grace." Thank goodness that Jesus is so faithful to run to our assistance when we humbly turn to Him in our moment of weakness! (Hebrews 2:18) He strengthened me once again with the promises of His word. As I surrendered the devil's lies to the truth of God's word, I found myself encouraged, and began to thank Him for His promises to me. I resisted the devil by saying, "Devil, you're a liar and a deceiver. My heart belongs to Jesus and I choose to believe Him." I continued, "Thank you, Lord, that You are causing my thoughts to be agreeable to your will and everything I put my hand to will prosper and succeed" (Proverbs 16:3). "You create in me the desire and power to carry out your will for my life" (Philippians 2:13). "You have anointed me to share and publish the Good News and Your word does not return void" (Isaiah 61:1-2; 1 John 2:20; Isaiah 55:11). That is

what it looks like to guard your heart from the enemy's lies, and fill it with the truth. Every time I turn my heart to Jesus and allow Him to fill my thoughts with His truth, I am set free from the devil's lies and their effect on my heart.

Once more, the devil had tried to deceive me with his lies so that I would quit and give up. He loves to distract us with busyness so that we won't accomplish what God has called us to do. That is his plan for me and it would have come to pass if I had chosen to believe his lies. When we look to Jesus and allow Him to expose the lies and replace them with His truth, we will experience God's plan and purpose for our life.

JESUS HAS COME TO RESCUE YOU AND SET YOUR HEART FREE FROM EVERY LIE OF THE ENEMY WITH THE TRUTH OF HIS LOVE.

Jesus wants you to live free from fear. He wants you to live free from a low self-image; free from insecurity; free from anxiety, discouragement, depression and every negative emotion that keeps you in bondage.

Read **Colossians 1:12-14**: *¹²Always thanking the Father... ¹³for he has rescued us from the one who rules in the kingdom of darkness and he has brought us into the Kingdom of his dear son. God has purchased our freedom with his blood, and has forgiven all our sins. NLT¹*

Why do we give thanks to the Father? What has Jesus rescued us from?

_____

_____

Isn't it wonderful to be part of a real adventure story? Jesus has rescued you from the devil's kingdom filled with darkness and lies. He's rescued you and brought you into His kingdom, full of light and love. He has forgiven all your sins and made you righteous by purchasing your freedom with His blood. So guard your heart above everything that you do. Don't let the devil corrupt your mind with his lies. Recognize the symptoms. When your heart feels negative emotions, turn to Jesus. Let Him fill your heart with the truth of His love, and live in the freedom He purchased for you.

What are the symptoms of believing the devil's lies?

_____

_____

What is the main truth the Holy Spirit revealed to you in today's study and how will you apply it to your life?

_____

_____

_____

_____

_____

♔ Day 3 ♔

AGREE WITH THE ONE WHO LOVES YOU

The spirit of the Lord God is upon me, because the Lord has anointed... me to preach... good tidings to... the poor...; He has sent me to... heal the brokenhearted, to proclaim liberty to the... captives and the opening of the prison... to those who are bound, to proclaim the acceptable year of the Lord [the year of His favor].

ISAIAH 61:1-2 AMP

Take time to pray before you begin.

Jesus said in these verses that He came to heal your heart with the Good News of his love and acceptance. Jesus came to tell you the Good News to set your heart free. He came to heal the broken places of your heart that have been caused by believing the lies of the enemy.

LISTEN TO THE WORDS OF JESUS IN JEREMIAH 31:3, 11 AND 14 (PARAPHRASED BY THE AUTHOR):

³I have loved you with an everlasting love, with everlasting kindness I have drawn you to myself and continued my faithfulness to you. ¹¹I have ransomed you and redeemed you from the hand of your enemy. ¹⁴I will fully satisfy your soul with abundance. I will satisfy you with my goodness."

Jesus paid for you with His blood. He ransomed and redeemed you from the hand of your enemy. The devil no longer has any right to your heart. Your heart belongs to Jesus.

Before you accepted Jesus as your Savior, you were a sinner. There was something wrong with you. When you accepted Jesus, your identity was changed. You became complete in Him (Colossians 2:9-10). You were made righteous. The devil used to be able to use your sins against you and tell you that you don't measure up because of your failures, but not anymore. Jesus took care of the sin problem. By His one sacrifice, all your sins were forgiven and you were made perfect in Him forever (Hebrews 10:14).

Jesus loves you with an extravagant, unfailing love and He wants your heart to be completely devoted to Him. He is the One Who loves you; His desire is to set your heart free with His love. He wants to satisfy your soul with abundance, and to fill your life with His goodness. He wants you to be rooted and secure in His love so that you might experience the fullness of life He has for you. He is waiting for you to give Him your heart so that His words of love can bring healing and wholeness to your soul.

How do you give your heart to the One Who loves you? How do you allow Him to dwell and make His permanent home in your heart so that you can be made whole with His love?

Let's look at **Ephesians 3:17** again: *May Christ **through your faith** [actually] dwell (settle down, abide, make his permanent home) in your hearts. May you be rooted deep in love and founded securely on love.* AMP

How does Jesus and His words of truth dwell and abide in your heart?

_____

_____

This scripture says that it is through your faith that Jesus is able to fill your mind, thoughts, and emotions with His love. The word *faith* in this verse comes from the Greek words *pistis* and *peitho*. *Strong's Concordance* defines faith (*Strong's*[4102]) as:

- ❧ Reliance upon Jesus for salvation
- ❧ To trust and believe
- ❧ To agree with

This verse says that when you believe Jesus by agreeing with what He says about you, you'll experience His love in the depths of your heart. He indwells your mind, your thoughts and your feelings and you experience freedom. You live free from fear, insecurity, unforgiveness, resentment, worry, doubt, offence, discouragement, and confusion when you agree with the One Who loves you.

Just as the lies of the devil produce negative emotions within your heart, the truth of what Jesus says produces positive emotions within your heart. You can always know when you are listening to the truth by how it makes your heart feel.

In **John 8:31-32** Jesus said: *If you abide in My word… you are truly My disciple. And you will know the Truth, and the Truth will set you free.* AMP

In **John 16:33** Jesus said: *I have told you these things, so that in Me you may have perfect [peace] and confidence.* AMP

In **John 15:11** Jesus said: *I have told you these things, that My joy and delight may be in you, and that your joy and gladness may be of full measure and complete and overflowing.* AMP

According to these verses, what emotions are produced in your heart when you listen and believe the truth of what Jesus speaks to you?

_____

_____

_____

_____

JESUS IS THE TRUTH

Jesus is the Truth, so every word He speaks is truth. When you agree with what He says about you, your heart will be full of perfect peace and confidence in Him. His words of love produce overflowing joy in your heart. **Psalm 119:162** says, *I rejoice in your word like one who finds a great treasure. NLT[1]*

We are either agreeing with the enemy's lies, or we are agreeing with the One Who loves us. Whom we agree with determines the condition of our heart and ultimately the fruit of our lives. So let's look for a moment at the words that Jesus speaks to us through God's Word.

JESUS' WORDS ARE TRUTH

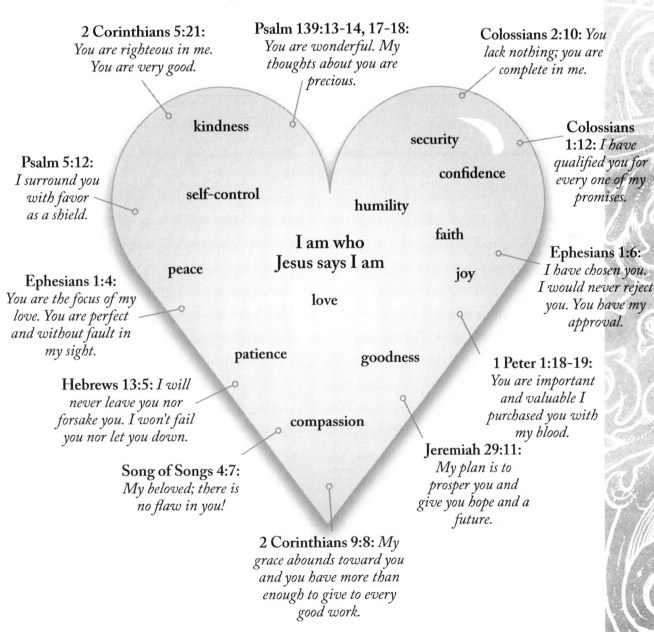

2 Corinthians 5:21: *You are righteous in me. You are very good.*

Psalm 139:13-14, 17-18: *You are wonderful. My thoughts about you are precious.*

Colossians 2:10: *You lack nothing; you are complete in me.*

Psalm 5:12: *I surround you with favor as a shield.*

Colossians 1:12: *I have qualified you for every one of my promises.*

Ephesians 1:4: *You are the focus of my love. You are perfect and without fault in my sight.*

Ephesians 1:6: *I have chosen you. I would never reject you. You have my approval.*

Hebrews 13:5: *I will never leave you nor forsake you. I won't fail you nor let you down.*

1 Peter 1:18-19: *You are important and valuable I purchased you with my blood.*

Song of Songs 4:7: *My beloved; there is no flaw in you!*

Jeremiah 29:11: *My plan is to prosper you and give you hope and a future.*

2 Corinthians 9:8: *My grace abounds toward you and you have more than enough to give to every good work.*

kindness · security · confidence · self-control · humility · faith · peace · I am who Jesus says I am · joy · love · patience · goodness · compassion

Jesus speaks His truth and promises to all of us. Have you ever wondered why some people simply receive the truth in their hearts and experience freedom, while others hear the same truth and continue to stay in bondage to the enemy's lies?

From a very young age, the enemy begins throwing his fiery darts (lies) at our hearts. When we accept his lies as truth, the darts penetrate our hearts and create brokenness.

THE LIE	YOUR AGREEMENT	BROKENNESS
You can't do it	I can't do it	discouragement
You're not good enough	I'm not good enough	condemnation
You're a failure	I'm a failure	shame
You're not as good as they are	I'm not as good as they are	jealousy
You lack in some way	I lack in some way	insecurity
You can't trust God	I can't really trust God	fear

This brokenness continues all our lives. Only the truth can set us free. My own heart was filled with brokenness and insecurity for many years because I believed the lies of my enemy. Because I agreed with the enemy of my soul, a negative picture was painted on the canvas of my heart, that said, *I'm not good enough. Something is wrong with me. I'm not as good as her. I lack in some way. They don't like me. I'm not as important as them. I don't qualify.* That was the picture that I had of myself. So, anytime I heard the truth such as *Connie, you're wonderful. You're beautiful. You're special. You're loved,* it just leaked right out of the holes in my heart. I couldn't receive it because my heart told me that it wasn't true for me. I had already decided in my heart that I didn't qualify.

LIES PRODUCE STRONGHOLDS.

A stronghold is a lie of the devil that you have accepted as truth. A stronghold was created in my heart because I agreed with the lies of the devil and those lies became what I believed was true about myself. The truth couldn't take root and produce God's promises in my life because I agreed with my enemy. Jesus taught this truth in Mark 4:1-20 in the parable of the sower. He taught that you can hear the Good News about what Jesus has done for you, but the enemy immediately comes and says, *that's not true for you,* and steals the truth from your heart, so it doesn't produce fruit.

You can hear the truth your whole life, but if you don't let go of the lies and begin to agree with the truth it will never heal your brokenness and make you whole. I came to a place in my life where the pain in my heart was so great I was willing to do anything to be free. One day, in desperation, I cried out to Jesus to, "Show me the truth that will set me free." In answer to my prayer, the Holy Spirit began to show me who I am in Jesus and that if I would just surrender my own opinion of myself and agree with His opinion of me, my heart would be made whole, and my life would be transformed. But the choice was mine: who was I going to believe? Who was I going to devote my heart to? Who was I going to agree with: the lies of my enemy or the truth of Jesus? With the help of the Holy Spirit, I made a decision that day to agree with the One Who loves me and a new picture of me began to be painted on the canvas of my heart. Today it looks like this: "I am loved, abundantly blessed, favored, protected, righteous, and free because of Jesus!"

I'd love to tell you that I only had to do that once, and it took care of everything, but the truth is, the lies still come and the devil still aims his fiery darts at my heart. Every day I have to make a choice between life and death. When I hear the lies of the devil and my heart feels the symptoms of those lies, I guard my heart by turning to Jesus and asking for strength to believe Him instead of the lie. I run to the throne of grace and agree with what Jesus says about me. A lie is only a temptation until you agree with it. When you put up the shield of faith by agreeing with the One Who loves you, the lie dissipates in the light of His love.

As long as you live you will continue to hear the lies, but as you continue to turn to Jesus your heart will say more and more, "No, that is not what is true about me. I am who God says I am because of Jesus." Jesus is your stronghold against the lies of the enemy. As you agree with the One Who loves you, your heart is made whole.

THE TRUTH	YOUR AGREEMENT	WHOLENESS
You can do it	I can do all things through Jesus	encouragement
You are very good	I am righteous in Jesus	peace
You're a success	I'm a success	joy
You're loved	I am loved	security
You are complete	I am complete in Christ	confidence
God is faithful	I can trust God completely	faith

Devote your heart to Jesus. Remember whomever you choose to agree with is the

one whose plan will come to pass in your life. Ephesians 3:20 says that God is able to bring His plan to pass in your life and do superabundantly far over and above your highest prayers, desires, thoughts, hopes or dreams when you begin to agree with the One Who loves you.

How can you experience the life of abundance Jesus has for you? How can you live free from the lies of the enemy and their affect on you?

_____

_____

_____

_____

_____

What is the main truth you received from today's lesson and how will you apply it to your life?

_____

_____

_____

_____

_____

Look at the heart on page 41 and take a moment to agree with the One Who loves you. Establish your heart in His love.

WEEK 3

An Oak of Righteousness

DAY 1:

The Greatest Gift of Love

DAY 2:

The Righteous Shall Live by Faith

DAY 3:

A Heart Established in Righteousness

[17] I pray that Christ will be more and more at home in your hearts as you trust in him. May your roots go down deep into the soil of God's marvelous love. [18] And may you have the power to understand, as all God's people should, how wide, how long, how high, and how deep his love really is. [19] May you experience the love of Christ, though it is so great you will never fully understand it. Then you will be filled with the fullness of life and power that comes from God! [20] Now glory be to God! By His mighty power at work within us, he is able to accomplish infinitely more than we would ever dare to ask or hope.

EPHESIANS 3:17-21 NLT [1]

☥ Day 1 ☥

THE GREATEST GIFT OF LOVE

The Spirit of God, the Master, is on me because God anointed me.
He sent me to preach good news to the poor, heal the heartbroken,
announce freedom to all captives, pardon all prisoners. God sent me to
announce the year of his grace — a celebration of God's destruction of our enemies
— and to comfort all who mourn, to care for the needs of all who mourn in Zion,
give them bouquets of roses instead of ashes, Messages of joy instead of news
*of doom, a praising heart instead of a languid spirit. **Rename them "Oaks of***
Righteousness" planted by God to display his glory.

ISAIAH 61:1-3 MSG

☥ *Take time to pray before you begin.* ☥

The above verses reveal that Jesus came to heal all the broken places of your heart with the Good News of His love. He came to proclaim your freedom from sin and set you free from the devil's lies that have held you in bondage. He came to tell you of a new covenant of grace and to celebrate the defeat of your enemy. He came to comfort you when you're sad and meet every need of your heart. He has done all of this by making you an **oak of righteousness**.

Fill in the blanks from the Scripture above:

Jesus came to give me _____ instead of ashes, messages of _____ instead of news of _____. A praising _____ instead of a spirit of despair; to change my identity from a sinner and rename me an **Oak of**_____; planted by God to display His _____.

The Message of Good News is the Gift of Righteousness

Read **2 Corinthians 5:17-21**: *[17]...anyone who belongs to Christ has become a new person. The old life is gone; a new life has begun! [18]And **all of this is a gift from God**, who brought us back to himself through Christ. And God has given us this task of reconciling people to him. [19]For God was in Christ, reconciling the world to himself, no longer counting people's sins against them. And he gave us this wonderful message of reconciliation. [20]So we are Christ's ambassadors; God is making his appeal through us. We speak for Christ when we plead, "Come back to God!" [21]For God made Christ, who never sinned, to be the offering for our sin, so that we could be made right with God through Christ.* NLT

2 Corinthians 5:21 reads: *[21] For He made Him who knew no sin to be sin for us,* *that we might become **the righteousness of God in Him.** NKJV*

The message of Good News that Jesus was sent to tell us in Isaiah 61:1-3 is revealed again in these verses. If you belong to Jesus, you have become a brand new person. You have been given a new identity. He sent others to tell you this wonderful Good News as well. He no longer counts your sins against you. By His one sacrifice, He became sin so that you and I could be made the righteousness of God in Christ. Being declared righteous in Him is His gift of love to you and to everyone who will receive it.

THE GREATEST DEMONSTRATION OF UNCONDITIONAL LOVE: JESUS PAID A GREAT PRICE TO GIVE YOU THE GIFT OF RIGHTEOUSNESS

Read **Isaiah 53:3-11**: *³He was despised and rejected — a man of sorrows, acquainted with deepest grief. We turned our backs on him and looked the other way. He was despised, and we did not care. ⁴Yet it was our weaknesses he carried; it was our sorrows that weighed him down. And we thought his troubles were a punishment from God, a punishment for his own sins! ⁵But he was pierced for our rebellion, crushed for our sins. He was beaten so we could be whole. He was whipped so we could be healed. ⁶All of us, like sheep, have strayed away. We have left God's paths to follow our own. Yet the LORD laid on him the sins of us all. ⁷He was oppressed and treated harshly, yet he never said a word. He was led like a lamb to the slaughter. And as a sheep is silent before the shearers, he did not open his mouth. ⁸Unjustly condemned, he was led away. No one cared that he died without descendants, that his life was cut short in midstream. But he was struck down for the rebellion of my people. ⁹He had done no wrong and had never deceived anyone. But he was buried like a criminal; he was put in a rich man's grave. ¹⁰But it was the LORD's good plan to crush him and cause him grief. Yet when his life is made an offering for sin, he will have many descendants. He will enjoy a long life, and the LORD's good plan will prosper in his hands. ¹¹When he sees all that is accomplished by his anguish, he will be satisfied. And because of his experience, **my righteous servant will make it possible for many to be counted righteous,** for he will bear all their sins.* NLT*

Make what Jesus did for you on the cross personal. Write your name on the lines below:

Verse 5: Jesus was pierced for _____ rebellion, crushed for _____ sins. He was beaten so _____ could be whole. Jesus was whipped so _____ could be healed.

Verse 11: When Jesus looks at _____ and sees what He accomplished for _____ on the cross by His one sacrifice, He is completely satisfied. Because of His experience, Jesus made it possible for _____ **to be counted righteous,** for He bore all _____ sins.

Do you really understand what Jesus did on the cross for you? You and I were sinners. We failed to meet God's requirements for righteousness. The Old Covenant said that we had to obey all of God's laws in order to be made righteous and worthy of God's promised blessings (Deuteronomy 6:25; 28:1-66), but we all failed and were declared sinners instead. According to the law, we deserve punishment for our sins and we were under the curse. But Jesus loves us so much that He came and took our place. He was beaten and you were made whole; He was whipped and you were healed. By His sacrifice, He rescued you from the curse of the law and gave you the gift of righteousness. (Galatians 3:13,14) He made you and me worthy of every promised blessing of God simply by receiving His gift of love.

Read **Romans 5:5-9:** *⁵Such hope never disappoints or deludes or shames us, for God's love has been poured out in our hearts through the Holy Spirit Who has been given to us. ⁶While we were yet in weakness [powerless to help ourselves], at the fitting time Christ died for (in behalf of) the ungodly. ⁷Now it is an extraordinary thing for one to give his life even for an upright man, though perhaps for a noble and lovable and generous benefactor someone might even dare to die. But God shows and clearly proves His [own] love for us by the fact that while we were still sinners, Christ (the Messiah, the Anointed One) died for us. ⁹Therefore... we are now justified (acquitted, **made righteous**, and brought into right relationship with God) by Christ's blood.* AMP

Make verse 8 and 9 personal. Write your name on the lines below:

God clearly proved His love for _____ by the fact that while _____ was still a sinner Jesus died for _____. _____ is now justified — acquitted, **made righteous** by Christ's blood.

What does it mean to be made righteous? *Righteous* means: "justified, acquitted, free from blame or guilt, holy, innocent." *(Strong's ¹³⁴², ¹³⁴³, ¹³⁴⁴)*

In being made righteous, you are justified. In order to get a clearer understanding of this amazing gift, let's look at the definition of *justification*:

*It is the judicial act of God, by which he pardons all the sins of those who believe in Christ, and accounts, accepts, and **treats them as righteous** in the eye of the law. In addition to the pardon of sin, justification declares that all the claims of the law are satisfied. The law is not relaxed or set aside, but is declared to be fulfilled in the strictest sense; and so **the person justified is declared to be entitled to all the advantages and rewards arising from perfect obedience to the law** (Romans 5:1-10). It proceeds on the crediting to the believer by God himself of the perfect righteousness, of Jesus Christ (Romans 10:3-9). Justification is not the forgiveness of a man without righteousness, but a declaration that he possesses a righteousness* *which perfectly and forever satisfies the law, namely, Christ's righteousness (2 Corinthians 5:21; Romans 4:6-8).[1]*

Do you see why righteousness is the greatest gift of love? Even though you and I do not deserve to be declared righteous because we fail at times, Jesus has given us His perfect righteousness. When God looks at you in Christ, He sees you as perfect, holy, innocent, and blameless because your sins have been forgiven and forgotten (Hebrews 8:12). God Himself declares you and me entitled to all the blessings and rewards of one who has perfectly obeyed the law even though we are guilty of many sins. It is finished! All you and I need to do is receive His gift of love.

Romans 5:16-17 says: *[16]Again, **the gift of God** is not like the result of the one man's sin: The judgment followed one sin and brought condemnation, but **the gift** followed many trespasses and brought justification. [17]For if, by the trespass of the one man, death reigned through that one man, how much more will those who receive God's abundant provision of grace and of **the gift of righteousness** reign in life through the one man, Jesus Christ.* NIV

One man's sin brought judgment and condemnation to everyone because everyone sinned, but the gift of God is righteousness through Jesus to everyone who will receive it. If you have accepted Jesus as your Savior, you're a new person. Be conscious every day that you are the righteousness of God in Christ. It's your new identity in Jesus. You no longer have to try to be righteous. It is a gift you must only receive. This gift gives you the very nature of Jesus and qualifies you for every promised blessing of God. Every one of God's promises are "yes and amen" in your life because you are the righteousness of God in Christ Jesus! (2 Corinthians 1:20)

Remember, you learned previously that every lie the devil throws at you is an attempt to deceive you into believing this one lie:

You're not who God says you are.

The truth is you only need to believe one promise to qualify for every promised blessing of God:

I am the righteousness of God in Christ Jesus!

---

[1]Reference: http://www.christiananswers.net/dictionary/justification.html: Bible Encyclopedia

YOUR OLD IDENTITY

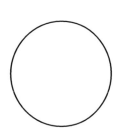

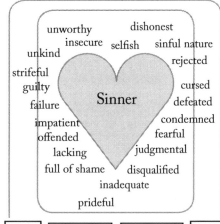

unworthy   dishonest

insecure   selfish   sinful nature

unkind   rejected

strifeful

guilty   cursed

failure   **Sinner**   defeated

impatient   condemned

offended   fearful

lacking   judgmental

full of shame   disqualified

inadequate

prideful

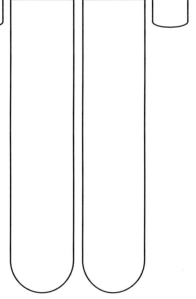

YOUR NEW IDENTITY IN CHRIST

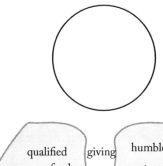

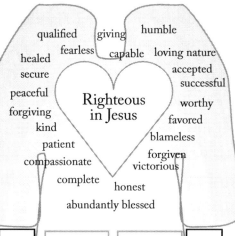

qualified   giving   humble

fearless   capable   loving nature

healed   accepted

secure   successful

peaceful   **Righteous**   worthy

forgiving   **in Jesus**   favored

kind   blameless

patient   forgiven

compassionate   victorious

complete   honest

abundantly blessed

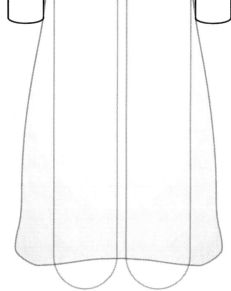

WHO ARE YOU?

What does your heart truly believe? Look back at the list of the characteristics of a sinner. The devil will try to convince you that you are still a sinner because of your failures. He wants you to believe the lie that *you are not who God says you are.* If you believe this lie, your life will produce the characteristics of a sinner, even though you truly are the righteousness of God in Christ Jesus. The belief of your heart will determine the fruit of your life.

Now look at the characteristics of the righteous. Jesus wants you to believe the truth that *you are the righteousness of God in Christ.* How does it make your heart feel to realize that these characteristics describe who you truly are in Jesus?

Jesus gave His name and everything He possesses to you as a gift. He took off your filthy sin-stained clothes and dressed you in a robe of righteousness. He clothed you with who He is. When He dressed you in His righteousness, He clothed you with approval, favor, forgiveness, abundant blessings, prosperity, health, kindness, love, success, and wholeness. Your Savior loves you so much that He did for you what you could never do for yourself. He gave you what you needed to qualify for every promise of God by giving you His perfect righteousness as a gift of His love. When you understand the magnitude of what Jesus accomplished for you in His finished work on the cross, you'll experience perfect peace in your heart in every situation. You'll rejoice in the truth that you are loved!

> **Isaiah 61:10** says: *I will sing for joy in God, explode in praise from deep in my soul! He dressed me up in a suit of salvation, he outfitted me in a robe of righteousness, as a bridegroom who puts on a tuxedo and a bride a jeweled tiara.* MSG

So rejoice in the One Who finished the work for you. You are dressed in a robe of righteousness. You have everything you need in Jesus. The next time you face a challenge and the devil attempts to deceive you with his lies, remember who you are. You can quench all his fiery darts, by rejoicing in this one truth and declaring, **"I am the righteousness of God in Christ Jesus!"** You are an oak of righteousness and when you agree with the One Who loves you, your life will display the glory of God.

What is the main truth the Holy Spirit revealed to you in today's study and how will you apply it to your life?

⫷ Day 2 ⫸
THE RIGHTEOUS SHALL LIVE BY FAITH

[17] This Good News tells us how God makes us right in his sight. This is accomplished from start to finish by faith. As the Scriptures say, "It is through faith that a righteous person has life."

ROMANS 1:17 NLT[2]

⫷ *Take time to pray before you begin.* ⫸

The Gospel is Good News. It is the message of God proving His amazing love for you and me by making us righteous in His sight through Jesus. This is accomplished from start to finish by faith. You learned previously that the word *faith* comes from the Greek word *pistis (Strong's [4102])* which means:

⫷ reliance upon Jesus for salvation

⫷ to trust or believe

⫷ to agree with God

The Bible says that the righteous shall live by faith. **2 Corinthians 4:13** says, *It is written: "I believed, therefore, I have spoken." With that same spirit of faith we also believe and therefore speak. NIV* Jesus made you an oak of righteousness. When your heart truly believes this truth, you'll confidently speak His promises over yourself and your family. Your roots will go down deep into the soil of God's marvelous love as you agree with the One Who loves you.

Read **Ephesians 3:17**: *I pray that Christ will be more and more at home in your hearts as you trust in him. May your roots go down deep into the soil of God's marvelous love. NLT[1]*

RIGHTEOUSNESS IS A FREE GIFT.

For quite a few years of my Christian life, I didn't live loved because I was trying to earn something that had already been given to me as a gift. I thought I had to do something else to truly be made righteous and worthy of God's approval and blessing. Unconsciously my heart believed that what Jesus did on the cross for me wasn't good enough, and I had to complete His work by adding something to it. I believed this lie of the enemy deep down in my heart, and it kept me in bondage for many years.

I was set free when the Holy Spirit began to reveal to me the Good News that you and I are already righteous because of Jesus. There is not one thing that we can add to what Jesus did on the cross to make us anymore righteous then we are right now. There are no "Five Steps to Answered Prayer," or "Four Steps to Pleasing God," "Three Steps to Prosperity," or even "Two Steps to Healing"! There is only one step and it's faith in Jesus, and when we trust in Him, we become righteous. That is what qualifies us for all the promises God has made to the righteous. They are our inheritance in Christ because of His great gift of love. He purchased them for us with His blood so that you and I could have peace in this world.

LET'S LOOK AT SOME OF THE PROMISES GOD HAS MADE TO THE RIGHTEOUS

<u>PROSPERITY</u> **Proverbs 13:21:** *Prosperity is the reward of the **righteous**. NIV*

<u>BLESSING AND FAVOR</u> **Psalm 5:12:** *For surely, O LORD, you bless the **righteous**; you surround them with your favor as with a shield. NIV* (Also see, **Deuteronomy 28:1-13**)

<u>FINANCIAL ABUNDANCE</u> **Psalm 37:17,19:** *The LORD sustains the **righteous**. [19]They will not be ashamed in the time of evil, and in the days of famine they will have abundance. NASB*

<u>BLESSED TO BE A BLESSING</u> **2 Corinthians 9:8-11:** *[8]God is able to make all grace abound to you, so that in all things at all times, having all that you need, you will abound in every good work. [9]As it is written: "He has scattered abroad his gifts to the poor; his **righteousness** endures forever." [10]Now he who supplies seed to the sower and bread for food will also supply and increase your store of seed and will enlarge the harvest of your **righteousness**. [11]You will be made rich in every way so that you can be generous on every occasion. NIV*

<u>DELIVERANCE</u> **Psalm 34:15,17,19:** *[15]The eyes of the LORD are on the **righteous** and his ears are attentive to their cry; [17]The **righteous** cry out, and the LORD hears them; he delivers them from all their troubles. [19]A **righteous** man may have many troubles, but the LORD delivers him from them all. NIV*

<u>A BLESSED FAMILY</u> **Proverbs 3:33:** *The Lord . . . declares . . . blessed (joyful and favored with blessings) the home of the just and consistently **righteous**. AMP*

<u>SAVED AND DELIVERED CHILDREN</u> **Proverbs 11:21:** *[The] seed of the **righteous** shall be delivered. KJV* (Also see, **Isaiah 59:21**)

<u>DESIRES GRANTED</u> **Proverbs 10:24:** *The desire of the **righteous** shall be granted. KJV*

<u>POWERFUL AND EFFECTIVE PRAYERS</u> **James 5:16:** *The prayer of a **righteous** man is powerful and effective. NIV* (Also see, **1 John 5:14-16**)

<u>PROTECTION</u> **Proverbs 12:21:** *No [actual] evil, misfortune, or calamity shall come upon the **righteous**. AMP* (Also see, **Psalm 91**)

Wow! What wonderful promises Jesus purchased for you and me! Does your heart really believe these promises are true for you? Do you really believe that you are the righteousness of God in Christ? How does your heart respond when you read these verses? Are you thankful for what Jesus made available for you? Or does your heart question God's love and promises? Remember, the righteous shall have true life by agreeing with the One Who loves them!

Just last year the economy began to decline and the news media was giving all kinds of bad reports about the financial state of our country. People were losing their jobs and there was fear in the hearts of many people. I remember very distinctly turning my heart to the Lord and asking, "Father, what do You say about this bad economy?"

The Holy Spirit reminded me of Psalm 37:17-19 which says that the Lord will take care of the righteous and in the time of famine they will have abundance.

What do you say about the righteous?" The Holy Spirit reminded me of Psalm 37:17-19 which says that the Lord will take care of the righteous and in the time of famine they will have abundance. I remember the peace that came over my heart as I thought upon this promise that Jesus purchased for me. I remember the Lord saying to me, "Many of my people don't see themselves as truly righteous in me so they won't believe what I say about them, and they won't experience the abundance that I provided for them through Jesus. But those who do believe will experience peace and abundance during this time of famine." I responded by saying, "Oh, thank You Jesus, for making me righteous. Thank You for loving me so much and giving me the grace to trust You! Thank You for your promise to take care of us during these bad economic times and blessing us with abundance. Your promise is an anchor for my soul. You are my peace and I love you, Lord."

Shortly after this conversation with Jesus, I was sitting on the back porch of my home with my entire family. My daughter-in-law began talking about how the economy was affecting the company she worked for and many people were being laid off. I encouraged her by reminding her that she is the righteousness of God in Christ and she has the favor and blessing of God because of Jesus. If she did get laid off, God would provide a better job for her. We have nothing to worry about because God's promise to the righteous during hard economic times is that we will have an abundance.

Now, I didn't always respond this way to God's promises to the righteous. Many years ago — when I didn't understand the amazing love God showed toward me by making me righteous in Jesus — the fruit of my life was fear and insecurity. Even though I had read this verse many times, my heart was unsure that God would really take care of me. I questioned God's promise instead of receiving it. I didn't live loved by Him by agreeing with what He said about me. Because of that, I experienced fear and lack instead of abundance. But it still didn't make the promise any less true.

Today, I guard my heart from the lies of the devil, by thinking daily upon how Jesus has made me righteous. My heart has become convinced of His great love for me. I'm not going to allow the devil to deceive me anymore by questioning God's promise of who I am in Jesus. I boldly shared with my entire family recently, that we are the righteousness of God in Christ Jesus and if God says we will experience abundance during the time of famine then that is exactly what is true for us. We don't look to the right or to the left and question God's promise because of what is happening around us. We are going to keep our eyes on Jesus and agree with the One Who loves us. We choose to trust Him and speak His word over our lives because we are righteous in Jesus, and *that is what it means to live by faith*. My family all agreed that we are blessed because of Jesus!

True to His word and promise, God has blessed my husband's business and it has grown by twenty-five percent; my son and daughter-in-law were both promoted in their jobs, and we experienced abundance during this time of "famine" because we are the righteousness of God in Christ Jesus! Woo hoo!

Take time right now to read back over the promises God has made to the righteous. Put your name in each verse and let His promises to you penetrate deep within your heart. Thank Jesus for each one.

How does thinking upon these promises make your heart feel? How do they reveal God's marvelous love for you? Which one ministers to your heart the most?

Let your roots go down deep into the soil of God's marvelous love by thankfully acknowledging these promises to be true for you and your family. You qualify because you are the righteousness of God in Christ Jesus! Remember the righteous shall live by faith. You can have peace in every situation by agreeing with the One Who loves you. You can live free from fear and insecurity by living loved by Him.

What is the main truth the Holy Spirit revealed to you in today's study and how will you apply it in your life?

✤ Day 3 ✤

A HEART ESTABLISHED IN RIGHTEOUSNESS

*You shall establish yourself in righteousness...: you shall be far from even
the thought of oppression or destruction, for you shall not fear, and from terror,
for it will not come near you.*

ISAIAH 54:14 AMP

❖ *Take time to pray before you begin.* ❖

You've previously learned that the devil's main objective is to deceive you into believing you're not who God says you are. His lies are intended to oppress you and cause you to experience fear in your heart. When your heart is established in righteousness however, Isaiah 54:14 above says the **thought of oppression will be far from you**. You may be tempted with a negative thought, but your heart will say, *No, that's not who I am. I am the righteousness of God in Christ Jesus, and His promises are true in my life*. Fear won't be able to take root in your heart when you know and believe who you are in Jesus.

HOW DO YOU BECOME ESTABLISHED IN RIGHTEOUSNESS?

Ephesians 4:23-24 says: *²³Instead, let the Spirit renew your thoughts and attitudes. ²⁴Put on your new nature, created to be like God—truly righteous and holy.* NLT²

How do you put on your new nature of righteousness? (Verse 23)

This verse shows you the importance of being constantly renewed in the spirit of your mind. By inviting Jesus into your thought processes and letting the Holy Spirit change the way you think, you will be strengthened in your faith and your heart will become established in righteousness.

The enemy is constantly trying to oppress us by filling our minds with his lies. If we believe them, we will live in bondage; he wants us to live in darkness. Just the other day I had a negative thought come into my mind about a particular person in my life. Immediately I recognized that thought as not being a part of who I am. I am the righteousness of God in Christ Jesus, and I have the mind of Christ (1 Corinthians 2:16). I invited Jesus into my thought process by asking Him, "Lord, help me see this person through your eyes and from your perspective." The Holy Spirit established my heart in righteousness and empowered me to see the best in this person, and the thought of oppression stayed far from me.

In another recent experience, my husband came to me with some bad news about his business. As he talked about the situation, I immediately turned my thoughts to Jesus and invited Him into my thought process, *Lord, I thank You that You are our Provider. You abundantly supply all of our needs. Thank You for making us righteous and surrounding us with favor as a shield. I trust You, Lord.* I then could tell my husband, "God will work it out for our good! We are blessed because of Jesus!" Fear didn't even have a chance to take root in my heart because my heart was established in righteousness and the thought of oppression stayed far from me.

Isaiah 32:17-18 says: *[17]The fruit of righteousness will be peace; the effect of righteousness will be quietness and confidence forever. [18]My people will live in peaceful dwelling places, in secure homes, in undisturbed places of rest.* NIV

What is the fruit and effect of being established in righteousness? (Verse 17)

What is God's promise to the righteous? (Verse 18)

When your heart is established in righteousness, the fruit of your life is peace and confidence forever! Your home is filled with peace and security. Your heart is undisturbed as you rest in the truth that you are loved!

Psalm 112:6-8 says: *[6]...a righteous man will be remembered forever. [7]He will have no fear of bad news; his heart is steadfast, trusting in the LORD. [8]His heart is secure, he will have no fear; in the end he will look in triumph on his foes.* NIV

When your heart is established in righteousness how will you react to negative circumstances, and what will be the end result?

This is the kind of life that Jesus died for you to live. He wants your heart to be established in righteousness, free from fear, and secure in His love. You have no fear of bad news because you know who you are and the promise you have in Jesus. When bad news comes, you respond by agreeing with the One Who loves you! You are victorious in every situation because you're the righteousness of God in Christ Jesus!

HOW A HEART ESTABLISHED IN RIGHTEOUSNESS RESPONDS TO BAD NEWS

BAD NEWS: *The economy is bad and people are losing their jobs.*

A HEART ESTABLISHED IN RIGHTEOUSNESS RESPONDS BY SAYING: "I am the righteousness of God in Christ Jesus! I prosper during famine. Thank you, Jesus, for taking care of me." (Psalm 37: 15-19)

BAD NEWS: *The weather is looking bad. A tornado may come near the area where you live.*

A HEART ESTABLISHED IN RIGHTEOUSNESS RESPONDS BY SAYING: "I am righteous in Jesus. No evil or calamity comes near my home. Thank You, Lord, for protecting me and my family." (Proverbs 12:21; Psalm 91)

BAD NEWS: *People are saying evil things about you.*

A HEART ESTABLISHED IN RIGHTEOUSNESS RESPONDS BY SAYING: "I am the righteousness of God in Christ Jesus! My righteousness shines like the noon day sun. Thank You, Jesus, that what You say about me is true. You think I'm wonderful!" (Psalm 37:6; Psalm 139:14-18)

BAD NEWS: *Your spouse is in a bad mood and is upset with you again.*

A HEART ESTABLISHED IN RIGHTEOUSNESS RESPONDS BY SAYING: "I am righteous in Jesus and my home is joyful and favored with blessings. Thank You, Lord, that You surround me with favor as a shield." (Psalm 5:12)

BAD NEWS: *You are experiencing symptoms of sickness in your body.*

A HEART ESTABLISHED IN RIGHTEOUSNESS RESPONDS BY SAYING: "I am the righteousness of God in Christ Jesus! I walk in divine health! Thank you, Lord, for forgiving all my sins and healing all my diseases." (Psalm 103:2,3)

BAD NEWS: *Your children are making poor choices.*

A HEART ESTABLISHED IN RIGHTEOUSNESS RESPONDS BY SAYING: "I am righteous in Jesus! My prayers for my children are powerful and effective. Lord, I can be very sure that You'll rescue my children (Proverbs 11:21). Thank You for working in their hearts and giving them the desire and power to do what pleases You." (Philippians 2:13).

> **Psalm 1:1-3** says: *¹Blessed (happy, fortunate, prosperous, and enviable) is the man whose... ²delight and desire are in the law of the Lord, and on His law (the precepts, the instructions, the teachings of God) he habitually meditates (ponders and studies) by day and by night. ³And he shall be like a tree firmly planted [and tended] by the streams of water, ready to bring forth its fruit in its season; its leaf also shall not fade or wither; and everything he does shall prosper." AMP*

How does God describe the person who is constantly thinking upon His word and the truth of who they are in Jesus?

Verse 1: _____

Verse 3: _____

This tree is a picture of who you are in Jesus and the kind of life that He came to give you. Invite Jesus into your thought processes daily by thinking upon the truth of who you are in Him. Let Him change the way you think about yourself and establish your heart in righteousness. You'll be like a tree planted by streams of living water, and your roots will go down deep into the soil of God's marvelous love. The Holy Spirit will bring out the fruit of righteousness in your life as you agree with the One Who loves you.

Remember when your heart is established in righteousness the thought of oppression will be far from you. You will not fear because you are secure in God's love!

Look at the illustration again. What is the main truth that stands out to you and how will you apply it in your life?

_____

_____

_____

_____

_____

_____

_____

_____

_____

WEEK 4

Living Securely in the Father's Love

DAY 1:
Living Securely in the Father's Love

DAY 2:
The Parable of the Father's Love

DAY 3:
Living as a Son or a Slave

*[17]May Christ through your **faith** [actually] dwell… in your **hearts**! May you be rooted deep in love and **founded securely on love**, [18]That you may have the power and be strong to apprehend and grasp with all saints [God's devoted people, the experience of that love] what is the breadth and length and height and depth of it; [19][That you may really come] to know [practically, through experience for yourselves] the love of Christ, which far surpasses mere knowledge… that you may be filled [through all your being] unto all the fullness of God…. [21]Now to Him Who, by… the [action of His] power that is at work within us, is able to [carry out His purpose and] do **superabundantly**, far over and above all that we [dare] ask or think [infinitely beyond our highest prayers, desires, thoughts, hopes, or dreams] —*

EPHESIANS 3:17-20 AMP

Day 1

LIVING SECURELY IN THE FATHER'S LOVE

May Christ through your faith [actually] dwell... in your hearts! May you be
*rooted deep in love and **founded securely on love**.*
EPHESIANS 3:17 AMP

Take time to pray before you begin.

Inspired by the Holy Spirit, the Apostle Paul prayed in Ephesians 3:17 above, that you would live securely in the Father's love. You are a child of the King and it delights His heart when you live loved by Him. The fullness of life Jesus came to give you is found in realizing how dearly you are loved by your Heavenly Father and allowing His words of love to change the beliefs of your heart.

WHAT DOES IT MEAN TO LIVE SECURELY IN THE FATHER'S LOVE?

Secure: "assured of one's good opinion of you; confident; free from fear or worry"
Insecure: "not sure of one's good opinion of you; not confident; beset by worry or fear"

We've all been insecure at times. Have you ever been concerned about someone's opinion of you? Have you ever feared being rejected? Has someone's negative attitude toward you ever caused your heart to feel anxious? I have experienced every one of these symptoms of insecurity. I have also experienced the freedom that comes by knowing who I am in Jesus and realizing that the only opinion that truly matters is my Heavenly Father's opinion of me. His perfect love sets me free from insecurity (1 John 4:18).

If your value comes from other people's opinions of you and whether or not they accept and approve of you, you'll always be insecure because their opinion can change from day to day. However, your Heavenly Father's good opinion of you never changes because you are in Christ. Jesus gave you His perfect righteousness, and you are just like Him in this world. (1 John 4:17)

Read **Ephesians 1:5-6**: *⁵For He foreordained us, (destined us, planned in love for us) to be adopted... as His own children through Jesus Christ, in accordance with the purpose of His will, [because it pleased Him and was His kind intent].* AMP

*⁶...to the praise of the glory of His grace, by which **He made us accepted in the beloved**.* NKJV

When you put your faith in Jesus, you became one with Him. It pleased the Father to make you His son or daughter through Jesus. In His perfect love, He made you fully accepted in the beloved! When Jesus was praying for us in

62

John 17:23, He said, *"Father, You love them, as much as You love me"*. NLT[1] This means that your Heavenly Father feels toward you the exact way He feels toward Jesus!

Read **Matthew 3:16-17**: *[16]After his baptism, as Jesus came up out of the water, the heavens were opened and he saw the Spirit of God descending like a dove and settling on him. [17]And a voice from heaven said, "This is my beloved Son, and I am fully pleased with him."* NLT[1]

If you are in the beloved, then the Father is saying the same thing about you. You are His beloved son or daughter and He is fully pleased with you because of your faith in Jesus.

Shortly after Jesus received His Father's complete approval and heard Him say, "You are My beloved Son," the devil came to tempt Him with the same lie he uses on all of us, *You're not who God says you are.* He questioned Jesus' identity. In **Matthew 4:3** the devil said, *"**If you are the Son of God**, change these stones into loaves of bread."* NLT[1]

Jesus resisted the devil by saying in **Matthew 4:4**, *"No! The Scriptures say, 'People need more than bread for their life; they must feed on every word of God.'"* (NLT[1])

In other words, Jesus was saying, "My identity comes from my Father's opinion of me. I choose to feed on every word He says about me. I am who my Father says I am!"

Not only did the devil challenge Jesus' identity, it was constantly being called into question by the people around Him. Jesus was continually being judged negatively, but His heart was secure in His Father's perfect love. Jesus didn't seek man's approval or worry about their opinion of Him because He lived loved by His Father.

JESUS IS OUR EXAMPLE OF WHAT IT LOOKS LIKE TO TRULY LIVE LOVED

Read what Jesus said in **John 5:30-32, 37, 41-42**: *[30]"But I do nothing without consulting the Father. I judge as I am told.... [31]If I were to testify on my own behalf, my testimony would not be valid. [32]But someone else is also testifying about me, and I can assure you that everything he says about me is true.*

[37]"And the Father himself has also testified about me....

[41]"Your approval or disapproval means nothing to me, [42]because I know you don't have God's love within you." NLT[1]

Jesus lived free from insecurity because He only let what the Father said about Him enter into His heart. Verse 30 reveals that He did nothing without consulting His Father. He asked, listened, and responded to every word He heard His Father say. He was so secure in His Father's love that man's approval or disapproval meant nothing to Him. All He focused on is what His Father said about Him, and He was convinced that everything His Father said was true. He lived free from the fear of

what others thought of Him because He was secure in His Father's approval. What His Father said about Him was all that mattered.

In **John 5:44** Jesus said, *[44]How is it possible for you to believe [how can you learn to believe], you who [are content to seek and] receive praise and honor and glory from one another, and yet do not seek the praise and honor and glory which come from Him Who alone is God?* AMP

Jesus was saying that if you value other people's opinion of you more than God's, you will never truly believe and trust Him. You'll live in insecurity your whole life if man's approval and acceptance is more important to you than God's.

Read **John 8:14-15, 25-26, 54, 55:** *[14]Jesus told them, "These claims are valid even though I make them about myself. For I know where I came from and where I am going, but you don't know this about me. [15]You judge me with all your human limitations...."*

[25]"Tell us who you are," they demanded. Jesus replied, "I am the one I have always claimed to be. [26]...I say only what I have heard from [my Father] and he is true."

[54]If I am merely boasting about myself, it doesn't count. But it is my Father who says these glorious things about me.... [55]...If I said otherwise I would be as great a liar as you!" NLT[1]

What a powerful way to live! What a wonderful example of what it means to live securely in the Father's love. Jesus showed us what it looks like to truly live loved. He knew the glorious things the Father said about Him were true, and He only said what He heard His Father say. Jesus agreed with the One Who loved Him. He realized that any opinion that isn't in agreement with His Father is a lie. He knew that if He said anything about Himself other than what His Father said He would be as great a liar as the men who were judging Him falsely.

I say only what I have heard from [my Father] and He is true.

I SAY ONLY WHAT I HEAR MY FATHER SAY

Take a moment to listen to the glorious things your Heavenly Father says about you in Christ: (write your name on the line below)

> My beloved _____,
>
> You are the apple of My eye, the delight of My heart, and I am fully pleased with you! My plans are to prosper you and give you a hope and a future. I've equipped you with everything you need to carry out My will. You are forgiven, righteous, capable, anointed, abundantly blessed, highly favored, qualified, complete, valuable, important, and free from all sin. You have the mind of Christ. I fully accept you and approve of you completely. Nothing can ever separate you from My love.
>
> Your Heavenly Father

When you live securely in the Father's love, man's approval or disapproval means nothing to you. You value God's opinion over any man's. You know who you are in Jesus, and you say only what you hear your Heavenly Father say about you. Now, if you were simply boasting about yourself, it would count for nothing, but these are the glorious things your Heavenly Father says about you in Christ, and what He says is true. Any other opinion is a lie. The next time the devil tempts you to question your identity in Christ, follow Jesus' example. Resist the devil's lies by saying, "I live by every word my Heavenly Father says about me. I am who my Father says I am because of Jesus!"

What did you learn today from Jesus' example, about what it means to live securely in the Father's love? How will it change the way you live?

_____

_____

_____

_____

_____

_____

_____

Day 2

THE PARABLE OF THE FATHER'S LOVE

Take time to pray before you begin.

In my journey of learning to live loved by my Heavenly Father, one of the things that has brought much peace to my heart is the truth that even when I fail, my Heavenly Father's opinion of me never changes. No matter how I may fall short, I can always run to Him and receive His love and forgiveness because He is never angry at me. He is always waiting for me to turn toward Him and establish my heart in His love once more.

Because the Old Covenant is full of stories of God pouring His wrath and anger on people because of their sin, many people have believed a lie which has caused them to misunderstand the Father's heart toward his wayward children. But we who have accepted Jesus as our Savior, are no longer under God's wrath (Romans 5:8-9; John 3:17-18). A New Covenant has been established through Jesus, and we no longer have to fear God's anger or judgment again. When we fail, He only feels compassion toward us because of His great love.

> Read **Isaiah 54:8-10**: *⁸"...with everlasting love I will have compassion on you," says the LORD, your Redeemer. ⁹"Just as I swore in the time of Noah that I would never again let a flood cover the earth, so now **I swear that I will never again be angry and punish you**. ¹⁰For the mountains may move and the hills disappear, but even then my faithful love for you will remain. My covenant of blessing will never be broken," says the LORD, who has mercy on you. NLT²*

What did God promise you in verse 9?

_____

_____

How will His heart always feel toward you? (Verses 8 and 10)

_____

_____

Your Heavenly Father gave you a promise in these verses. He said He would never again be angry with you because of your sins. His heart will always feel love and compassion toward you. You can live securely in His love.

Hebrews 12:5-11 teaches that your Heavenly Father will correct you when you do wrong, but because of His promise to you in Isaiah 54:9, you can be completely confident that He will never be angry at you.

Any time you sin it's because you've taken on a different opinion of yourself other than the one the Father has of you. You have forgotten who you are in Jesus. When you go your own way, the Father feels compassion toward you, and He corrects your wrong opinion of yourself.

There is a parable in the Bible, often called the "Prodigal Son," which would be better titled "The Parable of the Father's Love." This story clearly demonstrates our Heavenly Father's heart of love toward his wayward children. It's a beautiful picture of the unchanging, unconditional, constant love of a Father, even for his rebellious and disobedient son. Although the son was unfaithful, the Father's love for him never failed.

Read **Luke 15:11-24**: *¹¹There was a certain man who had two sons; ¹²and the younger of them said to his father, Father, give me the part of the property that falls [to me]. And he divided the estate between them. ¹³And not many days after that, the younger son gathered up all that he had and journeyed into a distant country, and there he wasted his fortune in reckless and loose [from restraint] living. ¹⁴And when he had spent all he had, a mighty famine came upon that country, and he began to fall behind and be in want. ¹⁵So he went and forced (glued) himself upon one of the citizens of that country, who sent him into his fields to feed the hogs. ¹⁶And he would gladly have fed on and filled his belly with the carob pods that the hogs were eating, but [they could not satisfy his hunger and] nobody gave him anything [better]. ¹⁷Then when he came to himself, he said, How many hired servants of my father have enough food, and [even food] to spare, but I am perishing (dying) here of hunger! ¹⁸I will get up and go to my father, and I will say to him, Father, I have sinned against heaven and in your sight. ¹⁹I am no longer worthy to be called your son; [just] make me like one of your hired servants. ²⁰So he got up and came to his [own] father. But while he was still a long way off, his father saw him and was moved with pity and tenderness [for him]; and he ran and embraced him and kissed him [fervently]. ²¹And the son said to him, Father, I have sinned against heaven and in your sight; I am no longer worthy to be called your son… [I no longer deserve to be recognized as a son of yours]! ²²But the father said to his bond servants, "Bring quickly the best robe (the festive robe of honor) and put it on him; and give him a ring for his hand and sandals for his feet. ²³And bring out the… fattened calf and kill it; and let us revel and feast and be happy and make merry, ²⁴Because this my son was dead and is alive again; he was lost and is found! And they began to revel and feast and make merry. AMP*

The younger son took his inheritance and wasted it on a sinful lifestyle. He had decided in his heart that going his own way would get him what he wanted. Just like Eve, he believed the lie that he lacked in some way and he was going to get his needs met outside of his relationship with his father. We have all, at one time or

another, been prodigal sons. We've all felt a sense of lack and looked outside of our relationship with God to meet our needs. We've all gone our own way and fallen short of the glory of God (Roman 3:12).

What was the result of the son going his own way and taking on his own opinion? (Verses 14-16)

_____

_____

_____

Sin is its own punishment. The Bible says the wages which sin pays is death (Romans 6:23 AMP). It wasn't the father's plan for the son to live with the pigs and be in want, but he loved his son enough to allow him the choice to live in his love, or to take on his own opinion and choose his own way. One hundred percent of the time going our own way will bring heartache and pain into our lives. We've all found ourselves at times eating with the pigs, our hearts filled with shame, condemnation, disappointment, and discouragement because we chose to believe the lie of our enemy instead of living in our Father's love. Our Heavenly Father has compassion toward us when we sin because he knows the shame sin brings and the pain it causes our hearts.

In verses 14-16 of the story above, we see that the son's poor choices eventually led him to lack and brokenness. He found himself hungry, sad, and rejected by all his friends. He finally came to realize that even the servants of his father's house had a better life than he did.

How did the son feel after he had sinned? What was his opinion of himself? (Verse 19)

_____

_____

HAVE YOU EVER BELIEVED IN YOUR HEART THAT YOU WERE UNWORTHY
BECAUSE OF YOUR FAILURES?

The son's opinion of himself was that he was *no longer worthy to be called a son.* Even though he believed the lie that he deserved to pay for his sins, that wasn't how his father felt.

When the father saw his wayward son from afar, what did he do and how did he feel toward him (Verse 20)?

_____

_____

_____

_____

What does this tell you about Your Heavenly Father's heart toward you when you turn to Him after you've done wrong?

_____

_____

From the father's perspective there was no condemnation, only unconditional love and compassion toward his son. He ran toward him and embraced him and kissed him fervently. The son must have been shocked. He had expected his father to be angry and hard on him, making him earn his way back into his graces. Even after the father had poured his love upon him, the son still believed in his heart that he was undeserving and unworthy to receive his father's blessing. The shame in his heart and the negative opinion he had of himself is revealed in these words which he spoke to his father, *"Father I have sinned against heaven and before you; I am no longer worthy to be called your son."* But what the boy expected, and what happened were very different things. In fact, the father didn't even acknowledge the son's sins. His focus was not on reprimanding him for wasting his inheritance, but rather, on reminding him of who he was, and restoring him to the honored position as his son.

The father said to his servants:

- *"Quickly, bring the best robe and put it on my son."* The robe was a symbol of honor. The father dressed his son with a robe of righteousness to remind him of who he is.
- *"Put a ring on his finger."* The ring was a symbol of authority. It meant he belonged to his father and everything the father had was his.
- *"Put shoes on his feet."* Slaves went barefoot, but sons wore shoes. This signified that he had not lost his position as the father's son.
- *"Kill the fatted calf."* A sacrifice was made to take away his sin and shame forever.

In the ancient world there was no way of preserving meat. When guests were invited for a meal, an appropriately sized animal was killed, enough to sufficiently feed the guests. For a small family a chicken or a pigeon would be adequate; for two families, a duck or a goose would be enough. If more people came, it would be appropriate to kill a goat or a lamb. The killing of a fatted calf was done only if the entire village was invited. This was indeed an event of great importance. It was a great celebration and meant that someone very special was being honored.

There was an even further significance to this killing of the fatted calf. The actual slaughter of the animal would take place in front of the doorway. When the guests would step across the blood of the slain animal, it was a sign that the past had been left behind. As the son, himself, stepped over the blood of the animal, he knew it meant he was completely forgiven and his past mistakes were forgotten. It was a sign

of his father's total and complete acceptance and forgiveness. The father welcomed him back unconditionally, his heart filled with joy as he honored his son.

Jesus used this story to give us a picture of the amazing love the Father has toward us! We've all failed at times and done things that we knew were wrong; we've all wanted to run and hide just like Adam and Eve did in the garden. Isn't it wonderful to know that when you fail, your Heavenly Father is watching and waiting for you to turn your heart toward him just like the father in this story did? He runs toward you to embrace you and fully accepts you as His beloved child. He removes the shame by reminding you of who you are in Jesus, and corrects your wrong opinion of yourself. He wants you to know that you are not defined by your sins or your past mistakes. You are defined by the truth that you are a royal son or daughter of the King and you are extravagantly loved by Him. Knowing this, you can live securely in His love.

Zephaniah 3:17: *The Lord your God is in the midst of you, a Mighty One, a Savior [Who saves]! He will rejoice over you with joy; He will rest [in silent satisfaction] and in His love He will be silent and make no mention [of past sins, or even recall them]; He will exult over you with singing. AMP*

What did you learn about your Heavenly Father's love for you in today's study? Why can you live securely in His love?

_____

_____

_____

_____

_____

_____

_____

⁘ Day 3 ⁘

LIVING AS A SON OR A SLAVE?

⁘ *Take time to pray before you begin.* ⁘

In the Parable of the Father's love, there were actually two sons: the younger one, whom we read about, and an older brother, who stayed behind with the father. Even though the older son didn't get lost in the world like his younger brother had, he was lost just the same. Only he was lost in self-righteousness, living life as a slave instead of a son, because he too had not yet learned to truly live loved by his father.

> Read **Luke 15:25-32:** *²⁵"Meanwhile, the older son was in the field. When he came near the house, he heard music and dancing. ²⁶So he called one of the servants and asked him what was going on. ²⁷'Your brother has come,' he replied, 'and your father has killed the fattened calf because he has him back safe and sound.'*
>
> *²⁸The older brother became angry and refused to go in. So his father went out and pleaded with him. ²⁹But he answered his father, 'Look! All these years I've been slaving for you and never disobeyed your orders. Yet you never gave me even a young goat so I could celebrate with my friends. ³⁰But when this son of yours who has squandered your property with prostitutes comes home, you kill the fattened calf for him!'*
>
> *³¹"'My son,' the father said, 'you are always with me, and everything I have is yours. ³²But we had to celebrate and be glad, because this brother of yours was dead and is alive again; he was lost and is found.'"* NIV

How did the older son feel when he heard about the father restoring and blessing his younger brother who had sinned? (Verse 28)

_____

How did he see himself in relationship to his father? (Verse 29)

_____

Why did the older son feel he was better than the younger son? (Verse 29 and 30)

_____

Why did the older brother condemn the younger brother and feel like he was disqualified to receive the blessing of his father? (Verse 30)

_____

_____

How did the Father correct his older son? (Verses 31 and 32)

_____

_____

The older son was a hard worker. He himself pointed out that while the younger son was out being rebellious and wasting his life, he remained faithful to his father. However, a closer look reveals that he wasn't living as a son who enjoyed a loving relationship with his father, but rather he saw himself as a slave trying to earn his father's love and approval. In verse 29 he said, *"I've been slaving for you."* He saw himself more as a faithful servant than a beloved son.

When the disobedient younger son returned home, the father had a great celebration and restored him to his honored position as his beloved son. The older son who was hard at work in the field, heard the rejoicing, and came in to investigate. When he saw the reason for the celebration, *he became very angry.* Not only was he furious because of the blessing his younger brother received from their father, he withdrew himself from fellowship with his brother. He felt his brother did not deserve to have others celebrating with him because of his poor choices. His brother needed to pay for his bad behavior. The father came to his older son to plead with him to come celebrate with the family and be restored to fellowship with his younger brother, but the older son's heart was filled with *disapproval and judgment.* He obviously had not spent time getting to know his father because he didn't understand His father's heart of unconditional love.

THE OLDER SON WAS GUILTY OF SELF-RIGHTEOUSNESS.

When the father came out to talk with his enraged son, the son immediately called the father's attention to all the wonderful things he had done for him over the years. In verse 29 he stated that he had never disobeyed one of his commands and had worked tirelessly for his father for years. This attitude sounds just like the proud Pharisee in Luke 18:9 whom Jesus described as *"certain ones who trusted in themselves that they were righteous, and viewed others with contempt."* Trusting in your good works rather than trusting in Jesus for your righteousness invariably results in a feeling of superiority over others. It causes a person's heart to be judgmental instead of compassionate toward those who have sinned.

The older brother became **jealous** of his younger brother because his father showered him with honor and blessings. In verses 29-30 he said, *²⁹"Look! All these years I've been slaving for you and never disobeyed your orders. Yet you never gave me even a young goat so I could celebrate with my friends. ³⁰But when this son of yours who has squandered your property with prostitutes comes home, you kill the fattened calf for him!"*

This hard working, faithful, devoted son, who never committed the type of sins that his younger brother did, still carried sin within his own heart. His heart was filled with anger, jealousy, self-righteousness and judgment because he was not truly living loved by his father. He didn't realize that it wasn't his hard work and devoted service that qualified him for his father's approval and blessing. Everything the father owned already belonged to him simply because he was his son.

Notice the words the father uses to correct his oldest son, *31"'My son,' the father said, 'you are always with me, and everything I have is yours. 32But we had to celebrate and be glad, because this brother of yours was dead and is alive again; he was lost and is found.'"* (Verses 31-32).

Notice the father doesn't reprimand his older son for his anger, jealousy, judgment, and self righteousness. He corrects him the same way he corrected his younger son; He simply reminds him of who he is. The father says, "You are my beloved son and everything I have belongs to you. Don't you realize how much I love you? This brother of yours was lost in his sin, but he has come back to the family. Come celebrate with us."

THE FATHER WAS INVITING HIS ELDER SON TO LIVE IN HIS LOVE

The Father knew that if his elder boy accepted the truth about his position as his son, all the anger, jealousy, judgment and self-righteousness in his heart would disappear. The relationship between him and his brother would be restored, and his heart would rejoice in his brother's blessing. When we live securely in our Heavenly Father's unconditional love and acceptance, we are free to extend that same unconditional love and acceptance toward our brothers and sisters in Christ.

Neither son was living loved because they didn't view themselves the way their father did. They both focused on their actions to determine whether or not they were worthy of their father's love. The younger son was condemned because of his failures. The older son was prideful because of his self-righteousness, and it caused brokenness in both of their hearts. Yet, the father patiently waited for both of them to simply embrace their true identity and begin to live loved by Him.

> *The father says, "You are my beloved son and everything I have belongs to you."*

I can relate to both sons. There have been times in my Christian life when my failures have made me feel unworthy of God's blessings. There have also been times when I tried so hard to please God through my "good works" and "faithfulness" that I judged those whom I felt were "unfaithful" to be unworthy of God's blessings. I have felt anger, jealousy, and judgment in my heart toward my brothers and sisters in Christ because I wasn't living loved by my Heavenly Father.

Today, I have learned to live securely in my Father's love and it has caused my heart

to be filled with love and compassion toward those who have not fully embraced who they are in Jesus. Jesus came to set us free from the slavery of sin. He came so we could live loved by the King.

> Read **Galatians 4:4-7:** *⁴But when the right time came, God sent his Son, born of a woman, subject to the law. ⁵God sent him to buy freedom for us who were slaves to the law, so that he could adopt us as his very own children. ⁶And because you Gentiles have become his children, God has sent the Spirit of his Son in your hearts, and now you can call God your dear Father. ⁷Now you are no longer a slave but God's own child. And since you are his child everything he has belongs to you." NLT* [1]

What security you can live in if you simply embrace the truth that you are a son or daughter of the King and everything He has belongs to you, because of Jesus. You no longer have to live as a slave trying to earn your master's approval and blessing by your "good works. "You can live loved by realizing that you already have your Heavenly Father's approval and blessing simply because you are His child. When you live securely in your Heavenly Father's unconditional love, you'll live free from sin. You'll be free to love others in the same way that He loves you.

What is the main truth the Holy Spirit revealed to you in today's study and how will you apply it to your life?

WEEK 5

Abundantly Free

DAY 1:
Abundantly Free

DAY 2:
The Devil Has Been Disarmed

DAY 3:
The Gift of No Condemnation

*[17]I pray that Christ will be more and more at home in your hearts as you
trust in him. May your roots go down deep into the soil of God's marvelous love.
[18]And may you have the power to understand, as all God's people should, how
wide, how long, how high, and how deep his love really is [19]May you experience
the love of Christ, though it is so great you will never fully understand it. Then
you will be filled with the fullness of life and power that comes from God!
[20]Now glory be to God! By His mighty power at work within us, he is able to
accomplish infinitely more than we would ever dare to ask or hope.*

EPHESIANS 3:17-20 NLT[1]

⁕ Day 1 ⁘

ABUNDANTLY FREE!

*⁷Because of the sacrifice of the Messiah, his blood poured out on the altar of the Cross, we're a free people — free of penalties and punishments chalked up by all our misdeeds. And not just barely free, either. **Abundantly free!** ⁸He thought of everything, provided for everything we could possibly need, ⁹letting us in on the plans he took such delight in making.*

EPHESIANS 1:7-8 MSG

⁘ *Take time to pray before you begin.* ⁘

As I read this passage of Scripture, the revelation of God's love fills my heart to such a degree, that tears fill my eyes. My heart is filled with love toward my Savior Who demonstrated such unconditional love toward me. Through His one sacrifice on the cross, Jesus set us free from all the penalties and punishments we deserve because of our failures. As a result, when we put our trust in Him, we don't have to pay for our sins anymore because He already paid the price for us. And we're not just barely free either, we're abundantly free! Free from the shame and condemnation that sin brings to our hearts. We're free to truly live loved by Him!

Condemnation is a negative opinion of yourself. It's the result of believing the devil's lie that you're not who God says you are because of your failures. It's that belief in your heart that you really don't deserve God's blessing because you haven't been good enough. Condemnation and shame bring fear to our hearts and cause us to question whether our Heavenly Father will really answer our prayers and fulfill His promises in our lives.

I used to live in condemnation because I believed the devil's lies. Shame was deeply imbedded in my heart. My heart was filled with fear because I was unsure of my Heavenly Father's opinion of me. But I no longer live there. Today I am free to receive His unconditional love and blessings because my heart believes the truth that there is no condemnation to those who are in Christ Jesus!

Read **Romans 8:1, 29-34** and **38, 39**: *¹Therefore, [there is] now no condemnation (no adjudging guilty of wrong) for those who are in Christ Jesus. AMP*

²⁹For those whom He foreknew [...and loved beforehand], He also destined from the beginning...to be molded into the image of His Son [and share inwardly His likeness], that He might become the firstborn among many brethren. ³⁰And those whom He thus foreordained, He also called; and those whom He called, He also justified (acquitted, made righteous, putting them into right standing with

Himself). And those whom He justified, He also glorified. ³¹What then shall we say to [all] this? If God is for us, who [can be] against us? [Who can be our foe, if God is on our side?] ³²He who did not withhold or spare [even] His own Son but gave Him up for us all, will He not also with Him freely and graciously give us all [other] things? ³³Who shall bring any charge against God's elect [when it is] God Who justifies [...Who puts us in right relation to Himself? Who shall come forward and accuse or impeach those whom God has chosen? Will God, Who acquits us?] ³⁴Who is there to condemn [us]? Will Christ Jesus... Who died, or rather Who was raised from the dead, Who is at the right hand of God actually pleading as He intercedes for us? AMP

³⁸And I am convinced that nothing can ever separate us from his love. Death can't, and life can't. The angels can't, and the demons can't. Our fears for today, our worries about tomorrow, and even the powers of hell can't keep God's love away. ³⁹Whether we are high above the sky or in the deepest ocean, nothing in all creation will ever be able to separate us from the love of God that is revealed in Christ Jesus our Lord. NLT¹

Make this passage of Scripture personal and let the truth penetrate deep within your heart. Put your name on the lines below.

Verse 1: There is therefore now no condemnation for _____. There is no judging me guilty of wrong because I am in Christ Jesus.

Verse 29: Because of God's great love for _____, He destined me to be molded into the image of Jesus and share inwardly His likeness.

Verse 30: He called _____to Himself. He justified and acquitted me. He made me righteous and also glorified me by making me one with Jesus.

Verse 31: If God is for me, who can be against me? Who can be my foe if God is on my side?

Verse 32: If my Heavenly Father did not even spare His own Son for me, then He will also freely and graciously give _____ all things.

Verse 33: Who shall bring any charge against _____ , when it is my Heavenly Father who justifies me? Who shall come forward and accuse me, when it is my Heavenly Father who has chosen me to be holy and without fault in His eyes?

Verse 34: Who will condemn _____? Will Christ Jesus who actually died for me so I could be free? Jesus is sitting at the right hand of my Heavenly Father actually pleading and interceding on my behalf!

Verse 38: I, _____, am convinced that nothing can ever separate

me from my Heavenly Father's love. Death can't and life can't, the angels can't, the demons can't, my fears for today, my worries about tomorrow, and even the powers of hell can't keep God's love away from me.

Verse 39: Whether _____ is high above the sky or in the deepest ocean, nothing in all creation will ever be able to separate me from the love of God that is revealed in Christ Jesus my Lord.

I have to just stop and say, "WOOHOO!" Jesus made it possible for you and me to live abundantly free from shame and condemnation by receiving our Heavenly Father's unconditional love toward us, and His good opinion of us in Christ. I love verse 33 in which Paul asks, *"Who can bring a charge against us?"* If our Heavenly Father, the King of kings, judges us justified, acquitted, innocent, and righteous, than no other judgment matters. He is the final authority in our lives. What He says about us is true!

Verse 34 says that Jesus is sitting at the right hand of the Father, actually pleading your case for you. Jesus is your advocate.

Read **1 John 2:1-2**: *¹My little children, I write you these things so that you may not violate God's law and sin. But if anyone should sin, we have an Advocate (One Who will intercede for us) with the Father—[it is] Jesus Christ [the all] righteous [upright, just, Who conforms to the Father's will in every purpose, thought, and action]. ²And He [that same Jesus Himself] is the propitiation (the atoning sacrifice) for our sins, and not for ours alone but also for [the sins of] the whole world.* AMP

The Apostle John was admonishing you in this verse not to sin, but if you do sin, Jesus is at the right hand of the Father interceding for you. His sacrifice was enough to free you from all condemnation. Even when you fail, He is constantly reminding you that you are righteous in Him.

One day while I was asking the Lord for a deeper revelation of this truth, an illustration of a courtroom scene came into my mind. It was so powerful and it helped me understand what it means for Jesus to be sitting at the right hand of the Father, interceding on my behalf.

The Father is the Righteous Judge (2 Timothy 4:8). The Bible says that the devil is your accuser (Revelation 12:10). He is the prosecuting attorney, but Jesus is your advocate. He is your defense attorney. He is sitting at the right hand of the Father, interceding for you, and you are seated with Him (Ephesians 2:6).

WRITE YOUR NAME ON THE LINES OF THE FOLLOWING COURT ROOM SCENE.

The devil throws his fiery darts at your heart. He takes the Law, the very Word of God and begins to accuse you by saying, "_____ is not righteous. The law says he/she has to keep all of Your commands perfectly in order to be declared righteous (Deuteronomy 6:24-25). _____ has failed so many times, he/she doesn't even come close to measuring up!"

Jesus is sitting at the right hand of the Father pleading on your behalf. He comes to your defense by saying, "Father, I am the atoning sacrifice for all of _____'s sins. The Law could never make him/her righteous. I love _____ so much that I died and rose again so that he/she could be declared righteous in Me. I fulfilled the law for _____ and gave him/her My righteousness as a gift of grace. _____is righteous because of _____'s faith in Me!"
(Romans 3:20-24)

The Father slams His gavel down on the desk and boldly states,
"_____ is declared righteous in my sight not because _____ has obeyed the Law perfectly, but because _____has placed his/her faith in my Son, Jesus."

The devil speaks up again with another accusation, "There are many conditions to Your promises and _____ has not met them all. The Law says _____ has to obey all Your commands perfectly in order to be blessed by you (Deuteronomy 28:1-14) and we all know _____ has failed to meet this condition. _____ does not qualify for your promised blessings!"

Jesus, your Advocate, defends you again, "Father, _____ is no longer a slave to the law and its demands upon him/her. _____ is your son/daughter and an heir to all of your promises. He/She qualifies for all your promised blessings because _____ has been made righteous through his/her faith in Me." (Galatians 4:4-7; Colossians 1:12-14)

The Father slams his gavel on his desk again and says, "_____ is My beloved son/daughter, and everything I have belongs to him/her. My promised blessings are 'Yes' and 'Amen' in _____'s life because he/she is in My Son, Jesus!" (2 Corinthians 1:20).

The devil makes one more attempt to accuse you and fill your heart with condemnation, "_____ is guilty of many sins. Yesterday, he/she argued with her spouse and was impatient with his/her children. _____ has made many poor choices in the past.

The Law says, 'If you do not obey every command of God, you'll be cursed (Deuteronomy 28:15-66). _____ deserves the curse. He/She must pay for his/her sins."

Sitting at the right hand of the Father, Jesus says, "Father, I purchased _____'s freedom from the curse of the law by becoming a curse for him/her (Galatians 3:13, 14). _____'s sins are forgiven and he/she is abundantly free from the penalty and punishments chalked up by his/her misdeeds (Ephesians 1:7). _____ is free from condemnation because of his/her faith in Me."

The Father slams his gavel down one last time and forever declares, "I don't remember a sin _____ ever committed (Hebrews 8:12). I have established a New Covenant with _____. Because of his/her faith in My Son, Jesus, I judge him/her forgiven, justified, innocent, acquitted, and righteous in Him. There is no condemnation to those who are in Christ Jesus!"

What a powerful illustration of what it means for Jesus to intercede on our behalf. The Father, Son, and Holy Spirit all agree that you have been made righteous and free from all condemnation through your faith in Jesus. The question is who are you agreeing with: your accuser or the One Who loves you? This is what determines whether or not you experience the freedom that Jesus purchased for you.

For many years of my Christian life, my heart was filled with shame because as a young teenage girl, I got pregnant before I was married. For seven years of my marriage, I struggled with discouragement and disappointment because of the devil's accusations. He spoke these lies to my heart, "You don't deserve a happy marriage because of the sin that you committed. You have to pay for your sin. God won't bless your marriage," and I believed his lies.

Yet, all the time, the Father, the Son and the Holy Spirit were agreeing that I had been forgiven and justified through my faith in Jesus. My freedom had been purchased with the blood of Jesus, but for years, I still lived in bondage to condemnation and guilt because I believed the lies of my accuser instead. My heart believed I was guilty as charged.

Do you see how a Christian who has been set free by being declared forgiven, justified, righteous and innocent by the King of kings can still live in bondage? It's because they agree with their accuser.

One day when I cried out to Jesus to "show me the truth that will set me free," the Holy Spirit began to give me a revelation of God's amazing love and grace. I heard the Lord speak these words to my heart, "Connie, I declare you justified. Your sins are forgiven and forgotten. You don't have to pay anymore. I made you righteous and worthy of all My promised blessings through your faith in Jesus! I paid the price for you to live loved! I paid the price for you to live free!"

Why can you and I live free from our past mistakes? Look at what the Lord says:

> [18]*"Forget the former things; do not dwell on the past. [25]I, even I, am he who blots out your transgressions, for my own sake, and remembers your sins no more."* (Isaiah 43:18, 25 NIV)

> [22]*"I have swept away your sins like the morning mists. I have scattered your offenses like the clouds. Oh, return to me, for I have paid the price to set you free."* (Isaiah 44:22 NLT [1])

As I surrendered the lies I had believed and embraced the truth of what my Savior did for me, my heart was set free from condemnation and my whole life was transformed. The more I thought upon the truth of who I am in Jesus and His great love for me, the more freedom I began to walk in. I began to experience the blessing of God upon my life as I began to agree with the One Who loved me.

Condemnation is the result of agreeing with your accuser. What are some of the lies the enemy has told you about yourself?

_____

_____

What does your Heavenly Father declare about you in Christ?

_____

Who do you agree with?

_____

Remember, who you choose to agree with will determine whose plan you experience in your life: bondage or freedom? The choice is yours! The price for freedom has already been paid. Live abundantly free from condemnation and experience God's abundant blessings upon your life by agreeing with the One Who loves you! Establish your heart in the truth by saying, "Lord, I agree with You! Thank You for setting me free from all guilt and condemnation. My sins have been forgiven and forgotten. I am righteous, justified, innocent, and acquitted from all the charges against me because of Your great sacrifice for me! I am free to live in Your love!"

What did you learn about living loved by your Heavenly Father in today's lesson and how will you apply it in your life?

_____

_____

_____

_____

✠ Day 2 ✠

THE DEVIL HAS BEEN DISARMED

I'm leaping and singing in the circle of your love; you saw my pain,
you disarmed my tormentors...
PSALM 31:7 MSG

Take time to pray before you begin.

Remember the courtroom scene from Day 1? What did the devil have in his hand to accuse you with and build his case against you? The devil uses the law to accuse you and to prove that you and I are not righteous nor worthy of God's blessing. If we were still under the law, his accusations about us would be true. The Good News is that we, who have accepted Jesus as our Savior, are no longer under the jurisdiction of the law; we are under God's grace (Romans 6:14). Our failures to uphold the law which our accuser has used against us have been nailed to the cross. Our prosecuting attorney has been disarmed. His evidence is not valid; he's just blowing smoke and has nothing on us. He can no longer accuse us of not being good enough, or deceive us with his lies when we know who we are in Jesus and what He accomplished on the cross for us.

> Read **Colossians 2:10-16, 18:** *¹⁰You also are complete through your union with Christ….¹¹When you came to Christ, you were "circumcised," but not by a physical procedure. Christ performed a spiritual circumcision—the cutting away of your sinful nature. ¹²For you were buried with Christ when you were baptized. And with him you were raised to new life because you trusted the mighty power of God, who raised Christ from the dead.*
>
> *¹³You were dead because of your sins and because your sinful nature was not yet cut away. Then God made you alive with Christ, for he forgave all our sins. ¹⁴He canceled the record of the charges against us and took it away by nailing it to the cross. ¹⁵In this way, he disarmed the spiritual rulers and authorities. He shamed them publicly by his victory over them on the cross. ¹⁶So don't let anyone condemn you. NLT²*
>
> *¹⁸Let no one defraud you by acting as an umpire and declaring you unworthy, and disqualifying you for the prize. AMP*

What is true of you through your union with Christ? (Verse 10)

When you came to Christ, what happened to your old sinful nature? (Verse 11)

You were once dead because of your sins. How did Jesus bring you to life? (Verse 13)

_____

_____

What did Jesus do with the record of the charges that were against you? (Verse 14)

_____

When Jesus won the victory for you on the cross, how did it affect the devil's accusations against you? (Verse 15)

_____

The devil uses the law to disqualify you. How do verses 16 and 18 encourage you to respond to his accusations or the accusations of others?

_____

_____

_____

You and I were once sinners. The law condemned us and proved that we were sinners because we failed to uphold God's commands. When we came to Christ, our old sinful nature was cut away from us and Jesus gave us a brand new righteous nature by forgiving all our sins. The record of the charges against us that proved we were sinners, was nailed to the cross. We are no longer defined by our failures. Instead, we are defined by our new nature in Christ. The devil has been disarmed because he can't use our failures against us anymore. When we receive God's forgiveness in Christ, it frees us from all shame and condemnation. Verses 16 and 18 admonish you to let no one condemn you! Let no one deceive you by disqualifying you for God's blessing. You have been qualified in Christ!

In order to live free from condemnation and the devil's accusations we must remember this truth when we fail. The devil is just waiting for you to fail so that he can come and accuse you again. He is hoping that you'll forget who you are and receive condemnation and shame in your heart.

One morning shortly after the Holy Spirit had revealed this wonderful Good News to me in Colossians 2:10-18, I had the opportunity to apply it to my life. While I was getting ready to teach Bible Study, I got very angry with my husband and began to argue with him. Suddenly, I realized I had fallen into sin by entering into strife with him. So I stormed out of his office, went into my bedroom and began to cry.

This incident was my accuser's opportunity to condemn me, and he began his accusations against me by saying, "Look at you! You don't qualify to teach Bible study. You just disobeyed God. You're a failure!" I thought about His accusations for

a moment, then I turned to Jesus and said, "Jesus, help me! I'm sorry I didn't trust You and I got into strife with my husband. Remind me one more time of the truth that sets me free."

At that moment **Colossians 2:13-18** came up in my heart, and the Holy Spirit reminded me that my failures, which had disqualified me for God's blessing, were nailed to the cross. The devil had been disarmed. His accusations against me had no merit: they were all lies.

The Holy Spirit ministered the truth to my heart and pointed me to Jesus.

I heard Him say, "Connie, your sins are forgiven. You are righteous in Me. You're qualified and anointed to teach God's Word because of who you are in Me. Don't let the devil or anyone else deceive you into believing that you are unworthy or disqualify you for my blessing." When I agreed with the truth, God's love set my heart free from condemnation.

When you live free from condemnation, you will be used by God to set others free as well. I remember boldly saying to the devil, "You have nothing on me! You are the one who is going to pay! I'm going to Bible Study today and teach those ladies that you have been disarmed. Your accusations against them are all lies. They are going to be equipped with the truth that the charges against them have been nailed to the cross. They will live free from condemnation by realizing they are forgiven and qualified in Jesus!" I felt so empowered to share this Good News with others!

We are no longer defined by our failures. Instead, we are defined by our new nature in Christ.

Later that day, my husband and I discussed in a peaceful manner the situation that had earlier made me angry. When I received God's forgiveness and walked free from condemnation, I was empowered by the Holy Spirit to forgive my husband and to love Him with God's love. The devil had lost and his plan did not come to pass in my life because I agreed with the One Who loves me. That's what it looks like to live loved and live free.

When you agree with the accusations of the devil and your heart is filled with condemnation, you will also agree with his accusations toward others. However, when you live free from condemnation by embracing your Heavenly Father's opinion of you, the main fruit of your life is love. You are empowered by the Holy Spirit to love others the same way that Jesus loves you. Your heart is free from all negative emotions toward yourself and toward others when it is filled with the truth that you are loved!

Have you recently been accused by the devil because of your failures?

_____

_____

How will you respond to him now that you realize he has been disarmed?

_____

_____

The next time you fail, and the devil begins accusing your heart, remember he has been disarmed. The charges he is making against you have been nailed to the cross. Receive God's forgiveness and remember that you are the righteousness of God in Christ Jesus. Live loved and live free by agreeing with the One Who loves you!

What did you learn today about what it means to live loved and live free, and how will you apply it in your everyday life?

_____

_____

_____

_____

_____

_____

_____

_____

_____

_____

⚜ Day 3 ⚜

THE GIFT OF NO CONDEMNATION

¹⁷For God did not send the Son into the world in order to judge (to reject, to condemn, to pass sentence on) the world, but that the world might find salvation and be made safe and sound through Him. ¹⁸He who believes in Him [who clings to, trusts in, relies on Him] is not judged [he who trusts in Him never comes up for judgment; for him there is no rejection, no condemnation—
he incurs no damnation].

JOHN 3:17-18 AMP

⚜ *Take time to pray before you begin.* ⚜

God did not send Jesus into the world to judge and condemn men for their sins. He sent Jesus so that the world might find salvation and freedom from sin through trusting Him. The Good News is that we who have put our trust in Jesus will never be judged and condemned by Him, and we can share this Good News with others.

For the last two days we have discussed a courtroom scene. We've learned that the devil is our accuser, and Jesus is our advocate. We'll end this week of study by reading a story from the Bible about a woman who was on trial for her sin. This passage of Scripture reveals Jesus' heart of love and grace toward those of us who have failed. His gift of no condemnation is made very clear. I pray it touches your heart as it has mine.

Read **John 8:1-11**: *¹But Jesus went to the Mount of Olives. ²Early in the morning (at dawn), He came back into the temple [court], and the people came to Him in crowds. He sat down and was teaching them, ³when the scribes and Pharisees brought a woman who had been caught in adultery. They made her stand in the middle of the court and put the case before Him. ⁴Teacher, they said, This woman has been caught in the very act of adultery. ⁵Now Moses in the Law commanded us that such [women—offenders] shall be stoned to death. But what do You say [to do with her—what is Your sentence]? ⁶This they said to try (test) Him, hoping they might find a charge on which to accuse Him. But Jesus stooped down and wrote on the ground with His finger. ⁷However, when they persisted with their question, He raised Himself up and said, Let him who is without sin among you be the first to throw a stone at her. ⁸Then He bent down and went on writing on the ground with His finger. ⁹They listened to Him, and then they began going out, conscience-stricken, one by one, from the oldest down to the last one of them, till Jesus was left alone, with the woman standing there before Him in the center of the court. ¹⁰When Jesus raised Himself up, He said to her, Woman, where are your*

accusers? Has no man condemned you? ¹¹She answered, No one, Lord! And Jesus said,
I do not condemn you either. Go on your way and from now on sin no more. AMP

What sin did the lady who was brought to court commit? (Verse 3)

_____

What did the scribes and Pharisees use to accuse and condemn her? (Verse 5)

_____

What did the law say she deserved? What was the penalty for her sin? (Verse 5)

_____

How did Jesus respond to the Pharisees who condemned this woman? (Verse 7)

_____

How did Jesus set her free? What did He say to her in verse 11?

_____

In these verses we see a perfect example of a courtroom scene. The Pharisees brought a woman caught in adultery before Jesus to be judged. Just like the devil, the Pharisees used the law to accuse her and prove that she deserved to be condemned for her sin. The law said that her punishment was to be stoned, and the religious leaders wanted to make sure she got what she deserved. They tested Jesus by asking, *"The law says she should be stoned to death, but what do you say?"* They all had stones in their hands. The stones represented the law which brings death (2 Corinthians 3:7). They were ready to pass the judgment of the law on her when Jesus spoke up and said, *"Let him who is without sin cast the first stone."* Jesus revealed a very important truth in this statement: only those who are without sin truly have the power and authority to judge someone else. You and I do not have the authority to pass judgment on anyone because we have all been guilty of sin. Neither does anyone else have the authority to pass judgment on us. The truth is all of us deserve to be punished according to the law, but thank God for Jesus!

Realizing that each one of them was guilty of sin, they all began to drop their stones (the law) and walk away. Jesus was the only one without sin. He was the only one that had the power and authority to judge this woman, and he didn't have a stone (the law) in his hand.

When Jesus and the woman caught in adultery were the only ones left in this court room, Jesus asked her this question, *"Woman, where are your accusers? Has no man condemned you?"* She replied, *"No, one Lord."* In calling Him Lord, she acknowledged her faith in Jesus. It was at this moment that Jesus revealed His heart of love and grace toward this woman.

John 1:17 says, *For while the Law was given through Moses, grace (unearned, undeserved favor and spiritual blessing) and truth came through Jesus Christ. AMP*

Jesus looked at this woman with love in His eyes and said, *"I do not condemn you either. Go on your way and from now on sin no more."*

JESUS SET HER FREE FROM THE PENALTY OF HER SIN BY GIVING HER THE GIFT OF NO CONDEMNATION.

When she received His gift of no condemnation for her sins, she then had the power *to go and sin no more*. Many of us have believed the lie that we first have to stop sinning in order to keep ourselves from being condemned, when actually the exact opposite is true. First we must receive the gift of "no condemnation to those who are in Christ Jesus," which then gives us the power to live a life free from sin.

Have you ever been condemned by yourself or others because of your failures? Has it given you the power to go and sin no more? No. Condemnation keeps you in the vicious cycle of sin. But God's grace sets you free from that cycle.

Have you ever felt condemned and unworthy because of a certain sin in your life? You may have an addiction, experienced an abortion, been through a divorce, committed adultery, struggled with overeating, mismanaged your money, or fallen into sexual immorality. Perhaps you are a person serving a prison sentence for a crime you committed; or you may just struggle with feelings of guilt and condemnation because of your failures.

The devil and the teachers of the law will accuse and condemn you by judging you unworthy of God's approval and blessing, but that's not the heart of Jesus toward you. Just like Jesus extended His grace toward this woman who was caught in adultery, He also extends His grace toward you. He wants you to live free from sin, so He offers to you the same gift he gave to this woman. As you stand before your Savior, let His words of love penetrate deep within your heart and set you free. Hear him say to you, "My beloved, I do not condemn you, go and sin no more."

How do Jesus' words of love and his gift of no condemnation affect your heart?

_____

_____

When you receive His gift of no condemnation, you are living loved. This is what empowers you to live free from sin (Romans 5:17). This is the kind of life Jesus came to give you! You are free to live loved by Him!

What is the main truth the Holy Spirit revealed to you as you read John 8:1-11? How will you apply it in your own life?

_____

_____

_____

_____

WEEK 6

Amazing Grace

DAY 1:
Amazing Grace

DAY 2:
Sin Has Lost Its Power

DAY 3:
Grace: The Power to Live Free from Sin

*16May He grant you out of the rich treasury of His glory to be **strengthened** and reinforced with mighty power in the inner man by the [Holy] Spirit…. 17May Christ through your **faith** [actually] dwell (settle down, abide, make His permanent home) in your **hearts**! May you be rooted deep in love and founded securely on love, 18That you may have the power and be strong to apprehend and grasp with all saints [God's devoted people, the **experience** of that love] what is the breadth and length and height and depth [of it;]19[That you may really come] to know [practically, through experience for yourselves] the love of Christ which far surpasses mere knowledge…: that you might be filled… [with] the **fullness of God** [may have the richest measure of the divine Presence, and become a body wholly filled and flooded with God Himself]! 20Now to Him Who, by (in consequence of) the [action of His] power that is at work within us, is able to [carry out His purpose and] **do super abundantly**, far over and above all that we [dare] ask or think [infinitely beyond our highest prayers, desires, thoughts, hopes or dreams]— 21To Him be glory in the church and in Christ Jesus throughout all generations forever and ever. Amen (so be it)!*

EPHESIANS 3:16-21 AMP

⟊ Day 1 ⟊

AMAZING GRACE

For while the law was given through Moses, grace (unearned, undeserved favor and spiritual blessing) and truth came through Jesus Christ.

JOHN 1:17 AMP

⟊ *Take time to pray before you begin.* ⟊

In my journey of living loved and living free, one of the things that has absolutely changed my life is the understanding of what it means to no longer live under the law, but rather to live in God's grace. The Bible says that the law condemns and kills, but the Spirit of grace gives life (2 Corinthians 3:6). At one time, we were all in bondage to the law, but Jesus came to set us free. The Bible says that the law was given by Moses, but something very different — grace and truth — came through Jesus Christ.

What was given by Moses? _____

What came through Jesus? _____

What does *grace* actually mean according to John 1:17 above:

_____

_____

The law requires that you earn God's blessing and favor through your perfect obedience to His commands, and then gives you what you deserve based on your actions. Grace, on the other hand, is the unearned, undeserved favor and blessing of God based on your faith in Jesus. **Galatians 5:1** says, *So Christ has really set us free ... don't get tied up again in slavery to the law. NLT* [1] Those who live under the law live in bondage, but those who learn to live in God's grace truly live loved and live free!

Read **Ephesians 2:1-10**: *[1]Once you were dead, doomed forever because of your many sins. [2]You used to live just like the rest of the world, full of sin, obeying Satan, the mighty prince of the power of the air. He is the spirit at work in the hearts of those who refuse to obey God. [3]All of us used to live that way, following the passions and desires of our evil nature. We were born with an evil nature, and we were under God's anger just like everyone else. NLT* [1]

*[4]But God — so rich is He in His mercy! Because of and **in order to satisfy the great and wonderful and intense love with which He loved us**, [5]Even when we were dead... by [our own] shortcomings and trespasses, He made us alive together in fellowship and in union with Christ;[... for] it is by grace (His favor and*

*mercy which you did not deserve) that you are saved (**delivered from judgment and made partakers of Christ's salvation**). ⁶And He raised us up together with Him and **made us sit down together [giving us joint seating with Him]** in the heavenly sphere [by virtue of our **being] in Christ Jesus.**... ⁷He did this that He might clearly demonstrate through the ages to come the immeasurable (limitless, surpassing) riches of **His free grace (His unmerited favor)** in [His] kindness and goodness of heart toward us in Christ Jesus. ⁸For it is **by free grace (God's unmerited favor)** that you are saved (**delivered from judgment and made partakers of Christ's salvation) through [your] faith.** And this salvation is not of yourselves [of your own doing, it came not through your own striving], but **it is the gift of God;***

*⁹Not because of works [**not the fulfillment of the Law's demands**], lest any man should boast. [It is not the result of what anyone can possibly do, so no one can pride himself in it or take glory to himself.] ¹⁰For we are God's [own] handiwork (His workmanship), recreated in Christ Jesus,...that we may do those good works which God predestined (planned beforehand) for us [taking paths which He prepared ahead of time], that we should walk in them [living the good life which He prearranged and made ready for us to live]."* AMP

Make this passage personal. Let the truth penetrate deep within your heart. Write your name on the lines below:

1 _____ was once doomed forever because of his/her many sins.

2 _____ used to live just like the rest of the world, full of sin, obeying Satan.

3 _____ was born with an evil nature and was under God's anger just like everyone else.

4 But God, so rich is He in His mercy, **in order to satisfy the great and wonderful and intense love** in which He loved _____ ,

5 Even when _____ was dead by his/her own shortcomings and sins, He made _____ alive together in fellowship and in union with Christ; **for it is by grace** (His favor and mercy which _____ did not deserve) that he/she is saved (**delivered from judgment and made partakers of Christ's salvation**).

6 And He raised _____ up together with Jesus and made him/her sit down together [giving _____ **joint seating with Him]** in the heavenly sphere [by virtue of _____ **being] in Christ Jesus.**

7 He did this that He might clearly demonstrate through the ages to come the immeasurable (limitless, surpassing) riches of **His free grace (His unmerited favor)**

in His kindness and goodness of heart toward _____ in Christ Jesus.

8 For it is **by free grace (God's unmerited favor)** that _____ is saved (**delivered from judgment and made partakers of Christ's salvation**) through his/her faith. And this salvation is not of myself [of my own doing, it came not through my own striving], but **it is a gift of God;**

9 Not because of works [**not the fulfillment of the Law's demands**], lest I should boast. [It is not the result of what I can possibly do, so I cannot pride myself in my good works or take glory in myself.]

10 For _____ is God's own handiwork (His workmanship) recreated in Christ Jesus, that _____ may do those good works which God predestined (planned beforehand) for him/her [taking paths which He prepared ahead of time], that _____ should walk in them [living the good life which He prearranged and made ready for _____ to live]."

What used to be true of your old nature before you came to Jesus? (Verses 1-3)

_____

_____

_____

How did God satisfy His great and wonderful and intense love for you? (Verses 4-6)

Verse 5:

_____

Verse 6:

_____

What did He demonstrate by doing this? Verse 7:

_____

How were you saved, delivered from judgment and given joint seating with Jesus? Did you earn your position in Christ by your obedience to the law? (Verses 8-9)

_____

_____

Look at verses 1-3 and verse 10 again. Explain the difference between the fruit of your old nature and the fruit of your new nature in Christ.

Verses 1-3:

_____

Verse 10:

_____

When I read this passage of Scripture, my heart is overwhelmed with love and thanksgiving toward Jesus for what He accomplished for you and me on the cross. The magnitude of His great, wonderful and intense love for us has become very real to my heart. You see, you and I used to be dead in our sins. We were doomed to failure and disappointment, with a sinful nature just like the rest of mankind.

But in order to satisfy his great, wonderful, and intense love, even when we were dead in our sins, Our Heavenly Father made us alive in Christ. By His grace — His unearned favor and undeserved blessing — He saved us from the judgment of our sins and raised us up together with Jesus. He gave us the position of highest honor by seating us with Jesus and making us one with Him. **Hebrews 12:2** says, _[Jesus] is seated in the place of highest honor beside God's throne in heaven. NLT[1]_ **Ephesians 2:6** says, _For he raised us from the dead along with Christ, and we are seated with him in the heavenly realms — all because we are one with Christ Jesus. NLT[1]_

This is your new position in Christ. Your Heavenly Father honors and esteems you in the very same way He honors and esteems Jesus because you have been made one with Jesus. You are in Him and He is in you (Galatians 2:20).

Imagine the throne of God, with Jesus sitting on the right hand of the Father in the highest place of honor, and you seated in Him because you have been made one with Him by the grace of God. You, too, are sitting in the highest place of honor in Christ.

WHAT DOES IT MEAN TO BE "IN CHRIST? WHAT ARE THE PRIVILEGES OF YOUR POSITION IN HIM?

Because you are in Christ Jesus, Ephesians 1:3 says you are blessed with every spiritual blessing in the heavenly realm. What are these spiritual blessings?

In Christ, you have a brand new nature of love. You are the righteousness of God in Him: 2 Corinthians 5:21

In Christ, you are holy and without fault in your Heavenly Father's eyes: Ephesians 1:4

In Christ, you are the beloved son or daughter of God: Ephesians 1:5

In Christ, you are highly favored, accepted and approved by the Father: Ephesians 1:6

In Christ, you are forgiven and redeemed: Ephesians 1:7

In Christ, you are free from shame and condemnation: Romans 8:1

In Christ, you're a joint heir with Jesus and everything the Father has belongs to you: Galatians 4:5-7

In Christ, you have received an inheritance: Ephesians 1:11

> **Ephesians 1:9,11:** *⁹God's secret plan has now been revealed to us; it is a plan centered on Christ… ¹¹because of Christ, we have received an inheritance from God. NLT¹*

> **Ephesians 3:6:** *And this is [His] secret plan: The Gentiles have an equal share with the Jews in all the riches inherited by God's children. Both groups have believed the Good News, and both are part of the same body and **enjoy together the promise of blessings through Christ Jesus.** NLT¹*

In Christ, the Holy Spirit empowers you to walk in righteousness: Ephesians 1:13,19-20

In Christ, every promise of God is *Yes,* and *Amen* in your life:
2 Corinthians 1:20

In Christ, the Father sings over you with joy. You are the delight of His heart:
Zephaniah 3:17

What does it do for your heart to realize that you have been placed in the highest position of honor in Christ? You are one with Jesus and a joint heir with Him to all the promised blessings of God because of His amazing grace!

———————————————————————————————————

———————————————————————————————————

Your Heavenly Father placed you in this highest position of honor to demonstrate His grace (His unmerited favor) and goodness and kindness of heart toward you in Christ. You did not earn this honored position through your obedience to the law and its demands on you, so you can't pride yourself in your good works. You were given this position as a gift of God's grace when you placed your faith in Jesus.

I used to believe that my obedience to God's law was what put me in a position of honor and qualified me for God's promised blessings in my life. Because of this kind of thinking, I was always striving to be good enough, continually looking for that one message that would give me the answer to what I needed *to do* in order to qualify. I saw myself as lacking instead of complete in Christ. Without realizing it, I had fallen for the same exact lie that Eve had, which was, *If you do 'this' you will be like God.* As a result, I was living like a slave trying to earn God's favor and approval, when all the time I was already seated in the highest place of honor in

Christ. My Heavenly Father had already made me just like Jesus through my faith in Him.

For years I lived under the Old Covenant of the law, trying to be made righteous through my good works, and it kept me in bondage, producing condemnation in my heart when I failed, and pride in my heart when I thought I was better than someone else.

Then I realized that my salvation (my new position in Christ) did not come through any action on my part; not my striving, not my good works, nor my fulfillment of the Law's demands. There was absolutely nothing I could pride myself in or take glory for; my new position in Christ was purely and completely a gift of God's grace — God's unmerited favor which I did not deserve. I came to see that I am God's masterpiece, recreated as a new person in Christ so that my life would produce good works (Ephesians 2:10), not through my own effort, but through the power of the Holy Spirit at work in me. You and I can live the glorious life Jesus has prepared for us when we begin to live our lives in God's grace.

Today I live loved by thankfully acknowledging my honored position in Christ. I agree with who I am in Jesus not because of anything I did to deserve it, but because of His gift of grace. And not only that, I am free to agree with who my husband, my children, my family, and my brothers and sisters in Christ are, too, because they have received the same gift as me. We are seated together with Christ in the highest place of honor as privileged sons and daughters of the King all because of the amazing grace and love of our Savior.

What did you learn today about your honored position in Christ? What did you learn about God's amazing grace?

_____

_____

_____

_____

_____

_____

_____

_____

⁂ Day 2 ⁂

SIN HAS LOST ITS POWER

For the wages of sin is death, but the free gift of God is eternal life through
Christ Jesus our Lord.

ROMANS 6:23 NLT[1]

⁂ *Take time to pray before you begin.* ⁂

When we begin to live loved by embracing our new position in Christ, sin loses its power in our lives. Sin destroys people's lives. It destroys families, relationships, our health, and our minds. **Proverbs 14:30** says, *envy, jealousy, and wrath are like rottenness of the bones.* AMP Sin has brought destruction into the lives of the people God loves since the beginning of time. From Adam and Eve until now we can see how the world is full of heartache and pain because that is the wage that sin pays; but God loved us so much that He sent Jesus to break the power of sin over our lives so we could live free in His grace.

Read the end of **Romans 5:18-21:**

> [18]*Yes, Adam's one sin brings condemnation for everyone, but Christ's one act of righteousness brings a right relationship with God and new life for everyone.* [19]*Because one person disobeyed God, many became sinners. But because one other person obeyed God, many will be made righteous.* [20]*God's law was given so that all people could see how sinful they were. But as people sinned more and more, God's wonderful grace became more abundant.* [21]*So just as sin ruled over all people and brought them to death, now God's wonderful grace rules instead, giving us right standing with God and resulting in eternal life through Jesus Christ our Lord.* NLT[2]

When Adam sinned it brought condemnation to everyone because we all inherited a sinful nature. But when Jesus obeyed God, He made it possible for you and me to inherit a righteous nature through our faith in Him. God's law was given to show us how sinful we were. Sin once ruled over us and brought us death, but now God's wonderful grace rules over us instead, giving us the gift of righteousness and eternal life through Jesus Christ, our Lord.

Now let's continue reading in **Romans 6:1-14:** [1]*Well then, should we keep on sinning so that God can show us more and more of his wonderful grace?* [2]*Of course not! Since we have died to sin, how can we continue to live in it?* [3]*Or have you forgotten that when we were joined with Christ Jesus in baptism, we joined him in his death?* [4]*For we died and were buried with Christ by baptism. And just as Christ was raised from the dead by the glorious power of the Father, now we also*

may live new lives. ⁵Since we have been united with him in his death, we will also be raised to life as he was. ⁶We know that our old sinful selves were crucified with Christ so that sin might lose its power in our lives. We are no longer slaves to sin. ⁷For when we died with Christ we were set free from the power of sin.

⁸And since we died with Christ, we know we will also live with him. ⁹We are sure of this because Christ was raised from the dead, and he will never die again. Death no longer has any power over him. ¹⁰When he died, he died once to break the power of sin. But now that he lives, he lives for the glory of God. ¹¹So you also should consider yourselves to be dead to the power of sin and alive to God through Christ Jesus.

¹²Do not let sin control the way you live; do not give in to sinful desires. ¹³Do not let any part of your body become an instrument of evil to serve sin. Instead, give yourselves completely to God, for you were dead, but now you have new life. So use your whole body as an instrument to do what is right for the glory of God. ¹⁴Sin is no longer your master, for you no longer live under the requirements of the law. Instead, you live under the freedom of God's grace. NLT²

I love this passage of Scripture. When some people hear the message of grace, and that we are made righteous, not through our obedience to the law, but through our faith in Christ, they often misunderstand it as an excuse to live in their old sinful nature. **Galatians 5:13** says, *you have been called to live in freedom — not freedom to satisfy your sinful nature, but freedom to serve one another in love.NLT¹* You and I are free to live loved and to love others with God's unconditional love. That's true freedom!

I personally don't want to have an excuse to act ungodly and live a brokenhearted life. I am convinced that the wages that sin pays is a broken heart and a broken life. I don't want to go down that path and find myself eating with the pigs. I want to agree with what my Heavenly Father says about me and find myself truly free from sin and its effects on my heart and life. I want to live in the freedom of having the power to truly obey God out of a heart that knows I am loved!

The Apostle Paul asked in verse 1, *Should we keep on sinning so that God can continue to show us more and more of His wonderful grace? Of course not! Since we have died to sin, how can we continue to live in it? NLT²*

Look at **Romans 6:6-7** again. What happened when your old sinful self was crucified with Christ?

Verse 6: _____

Verse 7: _____

How does Jesus want you to see yourself? (Romans 6:11)

_____

_____

Verse 6 says your old sinful self was crucified with Christ so that sin might lose its power in your life. You are no longer a slave to sin. When you died with Jesus, sin lost its power in your life because that's not who you are anymore. Your identity is no longer that of a sinner. Your old sinful self who was angry, offended, resentful, impatient, prideful, selfish, irritable, grouchy, jealous, judgmental, self-indulgent, and fearful died two thousand years ago on the cross with Jesus. You are better than that now! You were raised with Jesus to a brand new life of righteousness. You have a new nature that is loving, kind, joyful, patient, forgiving, humble, compassionate, faithful, self-controlled and peaceful. You are just like Jesus! (Colossians 3:5-15; Ephesians 4:21-32).When you and I consider ourselves dead to the power of sin and alive in Christ, sin loses its power in our lives.

What instructions did the Apostle Paul give you in Romans 6:12-13?

_____

_____

Read **Romans 6:14** again. Since sin is no longer your master and you no longer live under the requirements of the law, where do you live now? (Verse 14)

_____

Read **Titus 2:11-14**: _¹¹For the grace of God that brings salvation has appeared to all men. ¹²It teaches us to say "No" to ungodliness and worldly passions, and to live self-controlled, upright and godly lives in this present age, ¹³while we wait for the blessed hope—the glorious appearing of our great God and Savior, Jesus Christ, ¹⁴who gave himself for us to redeem us from all wickedness and to purify for himself a people that are his very own, eager to do what is good._ NIV

What does God's grace teach us and give us the power to do? (Verse 12)

_____

Why did Jesus give himself for you? (Verse 14)

_____

God's grace teaches us to say no to sin because it is not a part of who we are anymore. That is our old life that died with Jesus. Jesus gave Himself to purchase our freedom from sin and its evil deeds so we could live as sons and daughters of God, eager to do what is good.

The other day I was tempted to become very irritated with a particular person in my life, but God's grace has taught me to say no to sin. I remember thinking, _No, that's not who I am anymore, my old sinful self died with Jesus and sin has lost its power_ in my life. *I am the righteousness of God in Christ Jesus and I think only the best about this person. I have the mind of Christ.* I said, "Lord, thank You for Your grace that sets me free!" Immediately, I felt the power of God's grace working in my heart and I began to ponder on that which is good and lovely about them. I felt God's love rise up in my heart toward them. God's grace set my heart free from sin.

So I constantly take my heart to Jesus and ask for His grace.

I have been tempted to be jealous, offended, judgmental, and fearful at times. I know that if I allow sin in my heart by forgetting who I am in Jesus, it will bring heartache and disappointment into my life. So I constantly take my heart to Jesus and ask for His grace. He reminds me of who I am in Him and empowers me to say no to sin. I am consciously aware that negative thoughts and attitudes are not a part of who I am in Christ. You and I have been given a brand new life in Jesus. When we consider that we are dead to sin and alive to righteousness, sin loses its power in our lives. Grace empowers us to live free from all sin.

WHAT IS TRUE FREEDOM?

Read **Romans 6:15-23**: *¹⁵⁻¹⁸So, since we're out from under the old tyranny, does that mean we can live any old way we want? Since we're free in the freedom of God, can we do anything that comes to mind? ¹⁶Hardly. You know well enough from your own experience that there are some acts of so-called freedom that destroy freedom. Offer yourselves to sin, for instance, and it's your last free act. **But offer yourselves to the ways of God and the freedom never quits.** All your lives you've let sin tell you what to do. ¹⁷But thank God you've started listening to a new master, ¹⁸one whose commands set you free to live openly in his freedom! ¹⁹I'm using this freedom language because it's easy to picture. You can readily recall, can't you, how at one time the more you did just what you felt like doing—not caring about others, not caring about God—the worse your life became and the less freedom you had? **And how much different is it now as you live in God's freedom, your lives healed and expansive in holiness?** ²⁰As long as you did what you felt like doing, ignoring God, you didn't have to bother with right thinking or right living, or right anything for that matter. ²¹But do you call that a free life? What did you get out of it? Nothing you're proud of now. Where did it get you? A dead end. ²²**But now that you've found you don't have to listen to sin tell you what to do, and have discovered the delight of listening to God telling you, what a surprise! A whole, healed, put-together life right now, with more and more of life on the way!** ²³Work hard for sin your whole life and your pension is death. **But God's gift is real life, eternal life, delivered by Jesus, our Master.** MSG*

What kind of life does living in your old sinful nature give you? Reread the underlined portions of Scripture.

What kind of life does living in the freedom of who you are in Christ give you? Reread the boldface portions of Scripture.

_____

_____

_____

Sin brings brokenness, bondage and shame to your heart, but Jesus paid the price to set you free to live a whole, healed, put together life that's expansive in freedom. The power to live free from sin and its consequences is found in embracing the truth that you are dead to sin and alive to Jesus. Your sinful nature is dead and buried and your new righteous nature is alive and free.

Sin has lost its power in your life! Believe who you are in Jesus, say no to sin, and live in the freedom of God's amazing grace! Live loved and live free!

What did you learn today about sin's power in your life? How can you live free from sin?

_____

_____

_____

_____

_____

_____

_____

_____

_____

⁍ Day 3 ⁍

GRACE: THE POWER TO LIVE FREE FROM SIN

⁍ Take time to pray before you begin. ⁍

My life has been totally transformed by understanding the amazing love and grace of my Savior. I have taught on grace so many times, and yet this wonderful Good News never gets old. The more I think upon it, the deeper and wider my roots go down into God's amazing love for me.

I know what it feels like to live in the bondage of sin, my heart broken, trying desperately to satisfy my feeling of lack. There is nothing more disheartening than the pain of guilt and shame, and that low-grade fear that never seems to leave. I have also felt condemned one minute and self-righteous the next, putting up a good front for everyone to see, but believing that the real me was a failure underneath. I have known the frustration of blame-shifting and judging others, in a futile attempt to feel better about myself.

On the other hand, I know what it feels like to live in the freedom of God's grace, my heart whole, embracing the truth that I am complete in Jesus. There is nothing more exhilarating than freedom from all guilt and shame, and the perfect peace that passes all understanding. I love living free from condemnation and pride, realizing I've been made righteous in Jesus, knowing it has nothing to do with my good works. Because of God's grace, my heart has been filled with love and compassion toward others and a desire for them to know this same love of Jesus, so that they too, can live loved and free!

Our Heavenly Father knows the pain sin brings to the hearts of his sons and daughters, but He loves us so much that He made a way for us to live free — every single day — by receiving His amazing grace.

GRACE: THE DIVINE INFLUENCE UPON THE HEART AND ITS REFLECTION IN THE LIFE

In the New Testament, the word *grace* comes from the Greek word *charis (Strong's 5485)* Strong's concordance defines this word as, "the divine influence upon the heart and its reflection in the life." In other words, grace is the Holy Spirit's influence upon your mind, will, and emotions that causes you to reflect your new nature in Christ. **Hebrews 10:29** calls the Holy Spirit, *the Spirit of grace.*

In the Amplified Bible, **2 Corinthians 1:12** gives another wonderful definition of grace and how it affects your life: *the grace of God (the unmerited favor and merciful kindness by which God exerting His holy influence upon souls, turns them to Christ, and keeps, strengthens, and increases them in Christian virtues).*

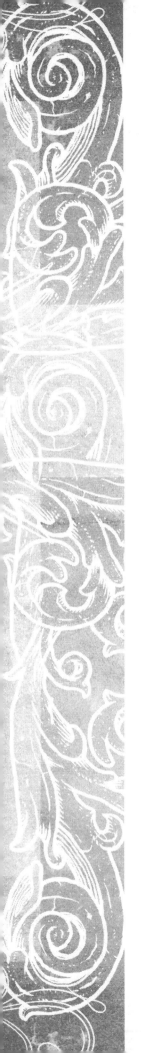

What a wonderful definition of grace. It is the Holy Spirit exerting His Holy influence upon your heart that strengthens you to believe the truth and brings out the fruit of righteousness in your life.

In the Old Covenant obedience was a requirement. You had to try hard to obey God. But in the New Covenant of grace, obedience becomes a promise. The Holy Spirit empowers you to obey God when you trust in His power within you. Look at what God promises to do in you through the power of the Holy Spirit:

> Read **Philippians 2:13**: "*[Not in your own strength] for it is God Who is all the while effectually at work in you [energizing and creating in you the power and desire], both to will and to work for His good pleasure and satisfaction and delight.*" AMP

> Read **Galatians 5:22-23**: "*²²But the fruit of the [Holy] Spirit [the work which His presence within accomplishes] is love, joy (gladness), peace, patience (an even temper, forbearance), kindness, goodness (benevolence), faithfulness, ²³Gentleness (meekness, humility), self-control (self-restraint, continence). Against such things there is no law [that can bring a charge].*" AMP

Do you have to struggle in your own ability to obey God and live free from sin? What promise do you find in Philippians 2:13?

_____

_____

What is the fruit that the Holy Spirit accomplishes in your life?

_____

_____

I used to struggle to do the right thing. I wanted so badly to obey God, but I always seemed to fail. I lived in the vicious cycle of sin and shame because I did not understand the power of God's grace that was available to me. One day the Holy Spirit revealed Philippians 2:13 to me and I realized that I didn't have to struggle anymore. As I agreed with the truth of who I am in Jesus, and looked to Him daily, He would create in me the desire and power to do what pleased Him. Every time I was tempted with a negative thought or attitude, I would take my heart to Jesus and pray, *Lord, thank You for creating in me the desire and power to do what pleases you.*

Trusting in my own effort and ability to obey God only led to failure, but when I began to trust in Jesus and the Holy Spirit's power within me, I began to see the fruit of the Spirit come out in my life. The Bible says that God gives His grace to those who are humble enough to receive it.

> Read **James 4:6-7**: "*⁶But He gives us more and more grace (power of the Holy Spirit, to meet this evil tendency and all others fully). That is why He says, God sets Himself against the proud and haughty, but gives grace [continually] to the*

lowly (those who are humble enough to receive it). ⁷*So be subject to God. Resist the devil [stand firm against him], and he will flee from you.* AMP

James 4:6 defines grace as, *the power of the Holy Spirit, to meet this evil tendency and all others fully.* Our old sinful nature has evil tendencies, such as:

- looking outside of God to meet needs within our heart
- getting angry easily
- being jealous and envious of others
- complaining and nagging
- worry and fear
- getting offended
- being judgmental and critical of others
- being prideful
- being slothful
- unforgiveness and resentment
- being impatient
- being irritable and grouchy

The devil wants to convince your heart that this is who you really are, but that's not true. Remember your old sinful self was crucified with Christ. That's not who you are anymore.

The Holy Spirit meets these evil tendencies. And when grace and sin meet, grace always wins! (Romans 5:21). Sin no longer has power in your life. 2 Corinthians 12:9 says that in your weakness, God's grace makes you strong!

Grace is the power of the Holy Spirit which enables you to overcome every temptation. Grace is not an excuse to live in sin. Instead it's the power of the Holy Spirit that enables you to live a life free from sin (Romans 6:1-14).

The one lie the devil is constantly tempting us to believe is: *You're not who God says you are.* He knows that what your heart believes will determine the fruit of your life. **Proverbs 23:7** says, *As [a man] thinks in his heart, so is he.* AMP

If you think you are still your old sinful self with evil tendencies, than you'll remain in bondage to sin. For example, your heart might say, *I have no self-control, I am an angry person. I am so disorganized. I don't have enough faith. I just can't seem to get it right. I can't seem to break free from this addiction. I will always struggle with* _____. **All sin is the result of not believing who you truly are in Christ.** As long as you hold onto that negative opinion of yourself, the vicious cycle of sin and shame will continue in your life, but God's grace is available to set you free.

When you feel negative emotions in your heart, remember the devil is tempting you to believe his lies. Take your heart to Jesus and receive His grace. Talk to Him about how your heart is feeling and ask Him to show you the truth that will set you free. When you humbly come to the throne of grace, the Holy Spirit will remind you of who you are in Jesus and empower you to believe the truth that sets you free.

> Read **Hebrews 4:14-16:** "*¹⁴Inasmuch then as we have a great High Priest Who has [already] ascended and passed through the heavens, Jesus the Son of God, let us hold fast our confession [of faith in Him]. ¹⁵For we do not have a High Priest Who is unable to understand and sympathize and have a shared feeling with our weaknesses and infirmities and liability to the assaults of temptation, but One Who has been tempted in every respect as we are, yet without sinning. ¹⁶Let us then fearlessly and confidently and boldly draw near to the throne of grace (the throne of God's unmerited favor to us sinners), that we may receive mercy [for our failures] and find grace to help in good time for every need [appropriate help and well-timed help, coming just when we need it].*" AMP

What does verse 14 admonish you to do?

_____

_____

This verse encourages you to hold fast to your confession of faith in Jesus: Who are you in Him?

SAY THE TRUTH OUT LOUD. ESTABLISH YOUR HEART IN THE TRUTH OF WHO YOU ARE IN JESUS:

I am a beloved son or daughter of God — I am valuable in Jesus — I am accepted in Jesus — I am approved in Jesus — I am special and important in Jesus — I am a joint heir with Jesus — I am complete in Jesus — I am seated in the highest place of honor in Jesus — I am righteous in Jesus — I am free from condemnation in Jesus — I am favored and abundantly blessed in Jesus — I am healed — I am a success in Jesus — I am an overcomer in Jesus — I am dead to sin and alive to righteousness in Jesus — Sin no longer has any power in my life.

The devil wants you to believe that none of this is true about you. Why does Jesus understand and sympathize with every temptation your heart feels? (Verse 15)

_____

_____

How can you overcome every temptation? (Verse 16)

_____

_____

Read **Romans 5:2,10,17**: *²Through [Jesus] also we have... access... by faith into this grace (state of God's favor) in which we [firmly...] stand. And let us rejoice and exult in our hope of experiencing and enjoying the glory of God.*

¹⁰For if while we were enemies we were reconciled to God through the death of His Son, it is much more [certain], now that we are reconciled, that we shall be saved (daily delivered from sin's dominion) through His [resurrection] life.

¹⁷... much more surely will those who receive [God's] overflowing grace... and the free gift of righteousness... reign as kings in life through the one Man Jesus Christ. AMP

The New Living Translation of **Romans 5:17** says, *all who receive God's wonderful, gracious gift of righteousness will live in triumph over sin and death through this one man, Jesus Christ.* NLT[1]

Romans 5:17 says that when we receive the gift of righteousness — who we are in Christ — and his overflowing grace — the power of the Holy Spirit — we will triumph over sin. We will reign as royal sons and daughters of the King through our faith in Jesus!

What did you learn about the grace of God in today's lesson? How can you live free from sin every day of your life?

_____

_____

_____

_____

_____

_____

_____

_____

_____

WEEK 7

Abiding in His Love

DAY 1:
Transformed by His Love

DAY 2:
Abiding in His Love

DAY 3:
The Prayer Jesus Prayed for Us

[16]I pray that from his glorious, unlimited resources he will give you mighty inner strength through his Holy Spirit. [17]And I pray that Christ will be more and more at home in your hearts as you trust in him. May your roots go down deep into the soil of God's marvelous love. [18]And may you have the power to understand, as all God's people should, how wide, how long, how high, and how deep his love really is. [19]May you experience the love of Christ, though it is so great you will never fully understand it. Then you will be filled with the fullness of life and power that comes from God. [20]Now glory be to God! By his mighty power at work within us, he is able to accomplish infinitely more than we would ever dare to ask or hope. [21]May he be given glory in the church and in Christ Jesus forever and ever through endless ages. Amen.

EPHESIANS 3:16-21 NLT[1]

⁅ Day 1 ⁆
TRANSFORMED BY HIS LOVE

⁅ *Take time to pray before you begin.* ⁆

There is no greater power in the universe than the power of love, and God is love! As we learn to live loved by Him, the power of His love will heal our hearts, transform our lives and bring glory to His name. You may have noticed that we've started each day of our Bible Study reading Ephesians 3:17-21. Today we'll take an in-depth look at this powerful chapter of the Bible.

> In **Ephesians 3:3,6,8,12** the Apostle Paul writes: *³As I briefly mentioned earlier in this letter, God himself revealed his secret plan to me. ⁶And this is the secret plan: The Gentiles have an equal share with the Jews in all **the riches inherited by God's children**. Both groups have believed the Good News, and both are part of the same body and **enjoy together the promise of blessings through Christ Jesus**. ⁸I was chosen for this special joy of telling the Gentiles about **the endless treasures available to them in Christ.***
>
> *¹²Because of Christ and our faith in him, we can now come fearlessly into God's presence, assured of His glad welcome.* NLT¹

What is God's secret plan? (Verse 6)

———————————————————————————————————

———————————————————————————————————

What was the Apostle Paul chosen to tell you? (Verse 8)

———————————————————————————————————

———————————————————————————————————

Because of Jesus and your faith in Him, what can you do? (Verse 12)

———————————————————————————————————

———————————————————————————————————

As I read Ephesians chapter 3 today, verse 8 in particular stood out to me. I personalized this verse as I often do when I'm reading Scripture, and let the truth of it soak into the depths of my heart. *The Apostle Paul was chosen for the special joy of telling Connie about the endless treasures available to her in Christ,* I thought. My mind immediately went to a wonderful illustration my friend Kelly used with the teenage girls in our Bible Study. She was teaching them about the inner beauty they have because Jesus lives inside them. She brought a jewelry box to our study, filled with hundreds of multi-colored crystal jewels. Although the outside was plain, the inside was strikingly beautiful as we gazed upon the precious treasures within the box. Each one of those gems represented a treasure we have in Jesus.

Thinking about that powerful lesson one more time and how it relates to today's study, I retrieved the jewelry box from my office mantle. Looking at the beautiful treasures it held, I was once again overwhelmed with the love of Jesus. Reaching inside, I picked up a pink gem, watching it glisten in the light. "Father," I asked, "which treasure in Christ does this one represent? Lovingly, I heard the Father say, "It represents my complete approval of you, my daughter. You don't ever have to look to another person again for approval because you have that treasure in Jesus" (Ephesians 1:6). Tears ran down my face as I pondered how that particular revelation of God's love has transformed my life.

Excited to hear Him speak to my heart again, I picked up a red jewel this time and asked, "Father, which treasure in Christ does this one represent?" He softly answered again, "It represents your value, my daughter. You don't have to prove your value through your performance or anything you do. I proved how valuable you are by paying for you with the blood of My Son, Jesus." (1 Peter 1:18-19)

There is no greater power in the universe than the power of love, and God is Love!

I could feel my heart being filled with the fullness of God's love as I picked up a purple gem "Show me once more, Father, what treasure in Christ does this one represent?" I asked. Again, "That one represents My gift of righteousness that qualifies you for all of My blessings," He answered (2 Corinthians 5:21). "You don't have to struggle to qualify any more, Connie. You can rest in My great love!" Taking in a deep breath, I pondered these treasures I have in Christ and the revelation of God's love within each one that truly sets my heart free. Reaching deep within the jewelry box, I scooped up as many jewels as my hands could hold. As I let them slip out of my fingers and back into the box, I prayed, "Thank You, Heavenly Father, You have given me so many treasures in Christ; Your love for me is so amazing! What a wonderful life journey I am on, daily discovering the treasures of Your love! I love You so much, Father!"

Sitting in God's presence, I picked up another handful of gems and gazed at them in my hand. The Holy Spirit continued to remind me of the endless treasures available to you and me in Christ: **Peace** (John 16:33); **Joy** (John 15:11); **Favor** (Psalm 5:12); **Protection** (Psalm 91); **Healing** (Isaiah 53:5); **Provision** (Philippians 4:19); **Wisdom** (Ephesians 1:8); **Guidance** (Romans 8:14); **Self-control** (2 Timothy 1:7); **Forgiveness** (Ephesians 1:7); **A Sound Mind** (2 Timothy 1:7); **Freedom from sin** (Romans 6:6,7); **The power of the Holy Spirit** (Philippians 2:13); **The Mind of Christ** (1 Corinthians 2:16); **Financial abundance** (2 Corinthians 9:8-11); **A Blessed Family** (Proverbs 3:33); **Blessed Children** (Psalm 112:2); **Acceptance** (Ephesians

1:6); **Deliverance** (Psalm 34:17-19); **A Heart of Love** (Ezekiel 36:26-27); **Security** (Romans 8:38-39); **The Gift of No Condemnation** (Romans 8:1); **Success** (Proverbs 16:3); **Strength** (Philippians 2:13)

Do you realize that every need and desire of your heart has been made available to you in Christ? You are truly complete in Him! His love fills every part of your heart with the fullness of God.

Now that you are aware of many of the treasures you have in Jesus, ask the Holy Spirit to reveal one that is particularly special to you, and write it on the lines below:

_____

_____

GOD'S LOVE FOR YOU IS REVEALED IN EACH TREASURE THAT HAS BEEN MADE AVAILABLE TO YOU IN CHRIST

Romans 8:39 says: *Nothing in all creation will ever be able to separate us from the love of God that is revealed in Christ Jesus our Lord. NLT[1]*

After revealing God's secret plan of the treasures made available to us in Christ, the Apostle Paul was inspired by the Holy Spirit to pray for each one of us to know and believe the love that Jesus has for us.

Read **Ephesians 3:14-21**: *[14]When I think of the wisdom and scope of God's plan, I fall to my knees and pray to the Father, [15]the Creator of everything in heaven and on earth. NLT[1]*

[16]I pray that out of his glorious riches he may strengthen you with power through his Spirit in your inner being, [17]so that Christ may dwell in your hearts through faith. And I pray that you, being rooted and established in love, [18]may have power, together with all the saints, to grasp how wide and long and high and deep is the love of Christ, [19]and to know this love that surpasses knowledge — that you may be filled to the measure of all the fullness of God. NIV

[20]Now to Him Who, by (in consequence of) the [action of His] power that is at work within us, is able to [carry out His purpose and] do super abundantly, far over and above all that we [dare] ask or think [infinitely beyond our highest prayers, desires, thoughts, hopes, or dreams] —

[21]To Him be glory in the church and in Christ Jesus throughout all generations forever and ever. Amen (so be it). AMP

What did the Apostle Paul pray that the Holy Spirit would strengthen you to do? (Verse 17)

_____

_____

In verses 6 and 8 in Ephesians chapter 3 the Apostle Paul revealed that He was sent to share the Good News of the promise of blessings we all have in Christ. He said the treasures available to us in Christ were endless. In verses 16 and 17, he prayed that the Holy Spirit would strengthen us in our inner man with the power to believe the Good News that He was sent to share with us. He prayed that we'd be strengthened so that Christ might dwell in our hearts through our faith in Him. He prayed that our thoughts and emotions would be filled with Jesus!

In verse 18, what did He pray that you would grasp?

_____

_____

Why did He pray in verse 19 that you would know the love of Christ?

_____

_____

As the Holy Spirit works in you and strengthens you to believe that you are loved, what is God able to do in your life? (Verse 20)

_____

_____

I have experienced great transformation in my heart and life as the Holy Spirit has continued to give me understanding of the riches I have in Christ. He also strengthens me in my inner man with the power to believe His great love for me. My journey in learning to live loved by Him, began by agreeing with the same simple prayer the Apostle Paul was inspired to pray, for you and me. Even now I often pray, "Lord, show me the truth that will set me free. Give me a deeper revelation of Your love for me. Strengthen me by Your grace to believe You."

It is only by the grace of God that we can grasp how wide, how long, how high and how deep the love of Jesus truly is for us. When our hearts are filled with His love, we are filled with the fullness of God. Every need of our heart is fully met. God is able to do exceedingly abundantly above our highest prayers, thoughts, hopes and dreams as we abide in His love.

I have experienced the transforming power of God's love, just as it's described in Ephesians 3:16-20 in so many ways. Let me share a personal example. In the early days of this ministry, I was very insecure about talking in front of people. Anytime I got an opportunity to teach Bible study, I would worry about what other people thought of me and whether or not I made any sense at all. Each time I'd finish teaching, I would look to people for their approval. If they didn't say anything, I'd think I must not have done a good job. If they did say something encouraging to

me, I would think they were just being nice. The enemy would come immediately with this lie, *You're so unqualified to teach anyone.* I would ponder his lies within my heart and it kept me in bondage to insecurity.

Finally, I got tired of being insecure, and I began taking my heart to Jesus concerning this fear. I asked Him to show me the truth that would set me free. The Holy Spirit began revealing to me the treasures I have in Christ:

- I am anointed in Jesus to set the captives free (1 John 2:20,27; Isaiah 61)
- I am qualified in Jesus to deliver the Good News of the gospel of grace (2 Corinthians 3:4-6)
- I can do all things through Christ Who strengthens me (Philippians 4:13)

These verses revealed the depth of Christ's love for me in this area of my life. As I pondered the truth in my heart, the Holy Spirit empowered me to believe it. Every time I was tempted to be afraid, I turned to Jesus and asked for strength to believe Him. I thanked Him for His promises of love to me. As a result, my heart has become established and secure in His love. Today I am free from insecurity in this area of my life. I feel empowered by the Holy Spirit to share the Good News of the treasures available to us in Christ.

As the Holy Spirit's power worked in my heart, God was able to bring His purpose to pass in my life. He equipped me to write Bible studies and books. He opened doors for me to travel around the nation and to Russia. He has used me to set the captives free. Now when I stand in front of people, I am very conscious of God's love for me and the treasures I have been given in Christ. God has done far beyond what I hoped or dreamed for in my life. As I have learned to live loved by Him, I have experienced the transforming power of His love.

You too, can experience the transforming power of God's love by thinking upon the treasures available to you in Christ. As you let them penetrate deep within your heart, the power of the Holy Spirit will work in you and you'll experience the freedom Jesus purchased for you.

What is the main truth the Holy Spirit revealed to you in today's lesson and how will you apply it in your life?

⊰ Day 2 ⊱

ABIDING IN HIS LOVE

⊰ *Take time to pray before you begin.* ⊱

WHAT DOES IT MEAN TO LIVE AND ABIDE IN THE LOVE OF JESUS AND HOW DOES IT AFFECT YOUR LIFE?

Today we'll study John 15:4-12 to discover the answer.

In **John 15:4-12** Jesus said: *⁴Dwell in Me, and I will dwell in you. [Live in Me, and I will live in you.] Just as no branch can bear fruit of itself without abiding in (being vitally united to) the vine, neither can you bear fruit unless you abide in Me. ⁵I am the Vine; you are the branches. Whoever lives in Me and I in him bears much (abundant) fruit. However, apart from Me [cut off from vital union with Me] you can do nothing. ⁶If a person does not dwell in Me, he is thrown out like a [broken-off] branch, and withers; such branches are gathered up and thrown into the fire, and they are burned. ⁷If you live in Me [abide vitally united to Me] and My words remain in you and continue to live in your hearts, ask whatever you will, and it shall be done for you.⁸When you bear (produce) much fruit, My Father is honored and glorified, and you show and prove yourselves to be true followers of Mine. ⁹I have loved you, [just] as the Father has loved Me; abide in My love [continue in His love with Me]. ¹⁰If you keep My commandments [if you continue to obey My instructions], you will abide in My love and live on in it, just as I have obeyed My Father's commandments and live on in His love. ¹¹I have told you these things, that My joy and delight may be in you, and that your joy and gladness may be of full measure and complete and overflowing. ¹²This is My commandment: that you love one another [just] as I have loved you.* AMP

What happens in your life when you depend upon yourself apart from Jesus?

Verse 4:_____

Verse 5: _____

Verse 6: _____

What happens in your life when you abide in Jesus?

Verse 5:_____

Verse 7:_____

Verse 8:_____

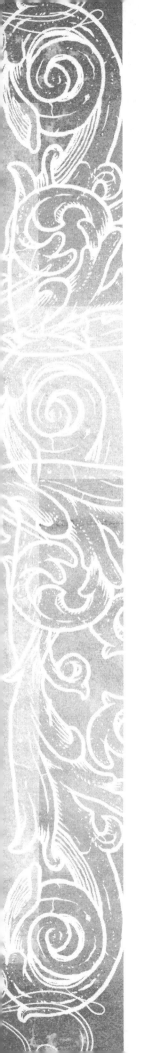

What fruit comes out in your life when you abide in Jesus? Read Galatians 5:22 and 23 on page 102.

_____

_____

Jesus is the vine and we are the branches. Just as a branch receives everything it needs to flourish and prosper from abiding in the vine, we too, receive everything we need to flourish and prosper through abiding in Jesus. He is our vital necessity. When we abide in Him we bear much abundant fruit, but apart from complete dependence on Him we can do nothing!

JESUS CLEARLY DESCRIBED TWO WAYS IN WHICH WE CAN LIVE

I can totally relate to verse 6 which reveals what happens to a branch that is not abiding in the vine. It does not flourish or prosper; it withers and gets burned. There have been times in my life when I have felt weak, brokenhearted, discouraged, disappointed and fearful because I was depending on either myself or someone else to meet my needs. When I look at myself apart from Jesus, I see myself as lacking in some way.

I can also relate to verses 7 and 8. When I abide in Jesus, thinking upon the treasures I have in Him, His word comes alive in me. I experience peace, joy, and love in my heart, and His promises in my life. When I abide in Jesus, I see myself as complete in Him!

What did Jesus tell you in verse 9?

_____

_____

Jesus told you He loves you just like the Father loves Him. He then said to continue to abide in His love. He showed you that the power to love others comes from receiving the Father's love for yourself.

What will the fruit of your life be if you abide in His love? (Verse 10)

_____

_____

What is His commandment? (Verse 12)

_____

_____

_____

Why did Jesus tell you to abide in His love? (Verse 11)

_____

_____

_____

When you read verse 10 which says, *If you keep My commandments... you will abide in my love,* you can mistakenly get the idea that Jesus is saying if you obey His commandments then He will love you. But the commandment Jesus is specifically referring to is found in verse 12, *This is My commandment: **that you love one another [just] as I have loved you.*** What Jesus is really teaching us in verse 10 is this: if you love others the way Jesus loves you, **you are** abiding in His love.

> Look at **John 15:9,10,12** again in the Message Bible: *⁹I've loved you the way my Father has loved me. Make yourselves at home in my love. ¹⁰If you keep my commands, you'll remain intimately at home in my love. That's what I've done— kept my Father's commands and made myself at home in his love. ¹²This is my command: Love one another the way I loved you.*

Let's recall together, the ways in which Jesus loves you:

- He forgives and forgets all your sins, and never brings them up again. (Hebrews 8:12)

- He does not condemn you nor judge you badly when you fail (Romans 8:1)

- He reminds you of who you are in Him and prays for you (Romans 8:29-34)

- He thinks only the best of you and rejoices in the truth about you (Zephaniah 3:17)

- He's never angry at you, but only feels love and compassion toward you (Isaiah 54:9-10)

- He is kind and patient toward you (1 Corinthians 13:4)

You can try to love people the way Jesus loves you, but apart from abiding in Him, you can do nothing! For many years I tried to honor, respect and love my husband; but in my own strength it was impossible. I found myself dwelling on his weaknesses and the areas he fell short. Any time I looked to him to meet my needs I always came up wanting. And the sense of lack I felt in my heart only produced the fruit of anger, frustration, resentment and disappointment toward him. I wasn't able to obey Jesus' command because I wasn't abiding in His love for me. Apart from Jesus, I could do nothing! I became like a withered up branch.

My heart changed when I began to live in Jesus and His love for me. Then I began to take the needs of my heart to Jesus, and He began to fill it with His great love. Instead of looking to my husband, I began to look to Jesus for approval,

provision, security, joy, peace, and unconditional love. As the needs of my heart are met in Him, I don't need to look to my husband anymore. God's love sets my heart free and empowers me to think on the good in my husband. My heart is filled with God's love towards him and I see him as righteous and blessed in Christ. Because Jesus loves both of us, we are blessed together in Him! I am now able to encourage him with the same encouragement the Holy Spirit has given me. Today, I think my husband is wonderful and I am truly blessed to have him in my life. I love him with all of my heart. Abiding in the love of Jesus transformed my heart and my marriage.

I now talk often to Jesus about His great love for me and think upon the endless treasures I have in Him — the promise of blessings that He purchased for me. It's during these moments that my heart is overwhelmed with His love because He has met every need and desire of my heart. This is what it means to abide in Jesus and remain intimately at home in His love.

Whenever I am tempted to feel irritated and frustrated with anyone, I take my heart to Jesus and let Him fill it with His love once again. I just have to refocus my attention on the One Who loves me and remember who I am in Him. When I abide in His love, my heart is filled with peace, and I am free to love others with His unconditional love.

You too, can live in the freedom of abiding in Jesus and His great love for you. Be conscious everyday that you are complete in Him. Thank Him for His love for you, and think upon the endless treasures you have in Him. Look to Jesus to meet every need of your heart; you won't need to look anywhere else. This will have a positive effect on every relationship in your life. You'll be filled up and overflowing with His love to such a degree that loving others the way He loves you will effortlessly flow from your heart. When you abide in His love, you'll bear much abundant fruit and your Heavenly Father will be glorified in you!

Have you ever looked to someone else besides Jesus to meet a need or desire of your heart? How did it affect your attitude toward that person?

_____

_____

What did you learn today about abiding in the love of Jesus? How will you apply it in your life?

_____

_____

_____

_____

_____

⟨ Day 3 ⟩

THE PRAYER JESUS PRAYED FOR US

⟨ *Take time to pray before you begin.* ⟩

I love watching Jesus interact with the Father in the gospels. He demonstrates such dependence and security in His Father's love. I want to live that way too. Jesus came to reconcile us into the very same relationship with the Father that He had. We are to live like Jesus in this world. He demonstrated what it truly looks like to abide in the Father's love through His prayer for us in John 17.

> Read **John 17:20-26:** *²⁰Neither for these alone do I pray [it is not for their sake only that I make this request], but also for all those who will ever come to believe in (trust in, cling to, rely on) Me through their word and teaching, ²¹That they all may be one, [just] as You, Father, are in Me and I in You, that they also may be one in Us, so that the world may believe and be convinced that You have sent Me. ²²I have given to them the glory and honor which You have given Me, that they may be one [even] as We are one: ²³I in them and You in Me, in order that they may become one and perfectly united, that the world may know and [definitely] recognize that You sent Me and that You have loved them [even] as You have loved Me. ²⁴Father, I desire that they also whom You have entrusted to Me [as Your gift to Me] may be with Me where I am, so that they may see My glory, which You have given Me [Your love gift to Me]; for You loved Me before the foundation of the world. ²⁵O just and righteous Father, although the world has not known You and has failed to recognize You and has never acknowledged You, I have known You [continually]; and these men understand and know that You have sent Me. ²⁶I have made Your Name known to them and revealed Your character and Your very Self, and I will continue to make [You] known, that the love which You have bestowed upon Me may be in them [felt in their hearts] and that I [Myself] may be in them. AMP*

What intimacy the Son had with the Father! Jesus established His heart in His Father's love by acknowledging the truth about their relationship. In His prayer, Jesus showed us what it looks like to abide in His Father's love. Let's take a look:

1. Jesus talked to His Father about their oneness and intimacy. In verse 21 He said, *"You, Father, are in Me and I in You."*

2. Jesus received the gift of His Father's glory which was the Father's gift of love to His Son. In verse 24 He said, *²⁴ "Father, I desire that they...may be with Me where I am, so that they may see My glory, which You have given Me [Your love gift to Me];"*

3. Jesus acknowledged that the Father loved Him. In verse 24 He said, *"Father,...You loved me before the foundation of the world."*

The wonderful Good News is that in His prayer Jesus revealed the Father's plan to bring you and me into the intimacy of their love relationship by making us one with them, and one with each other.

What did Jesus pray for you and me in verse 21?

_____

_____

_____

Jesus prayed that you and I would be one with each other, just as He and His Father are one; that we may also be one with them so that the world would believe that He is real.

Read part of Jesus prayer in **John 17** out of the Message Bible:

¹⁰Everything mine is yours, and yours mine, and my life is on display in them. ¹¹For I'm no longer going to be visible in the world; they'll continue in the world while I return to you. Holy Father, guard them as they pursue this life that you conferred as a gift through me, so they can be one heart and mind as we are one heart and mind. ¹⁵I'm not asking that you take them out of the world but that you guard them from the Evil One. ¹⁶They are no more defined by the world than I am defined by the world. ¹⁷Make them holy — consecrated — with the truth; your word is consecrating truth.

Because we are one with the Son and the Father, everything we have is His and everything He has is ours (Galatians 4:7). Jesus said that just as the world did not define Him, the world and its opinions and judgments does not define us either. The world gains its identity by seeking the good opinion of others, but our identity comes from the good opinion of our Heavenly Father. We are defined by the truth of who we are in Jesus.

In verse 22, what did Jesus reveal that He has given to you and me? And why?

_____

_____

_____

What did Jesus mean when He said that He had given us His glory and honor, the same glory and honor that the Father has given him? The word *glory* in this verse come from the Greek words *Doxa (Strong's ¹³⁹¹)* and *Doxazo (Strong's ¹³⁹²)*. According to the *Lexical Aids of the New Testament* these words mean:

- All that is excellent in the divine nature
- The image and character of God

- The opinion which one forms is to recognize, honor, praise, invest with dignity, give anyone esteem or honor by putting him into an honorable position

- The revelation and manifestation of all that God is and has

- God's self-revelation in which He manifests all the goodness that He is.

When Jesus gave us His glory, He gave us everything that is excellent in His divine nature. He gave us His very character; His perfect righteousness. The good opinion that the Father had of Jesus, Jesus gave to us. He gave us the same honored position His Father gave to Him by making us one with Himself.

Why did He give us His glory and honor?

Verse 22:_____

Verse 23:_____

Jesus gave His honored position to each of us so that we could truly be one and perfectly united in heart and mind. Jesus is in us and the Father is in Jesus and we are all one in Him. He did this so the whole world would know that the Father loves us as much as He loves Jesus.

When He gave us His glory, He made us all just like Himself. He gave each of us His very character; His very nature. He made us all just as valuable, important, special, anointed, approved and righteous as Himself. We are all a part of God's family by virtue of our being in Christ Jesus. We will no longer feel superior or inferior toward each other when we realize that we are all just like Jesus in this world. When we compare ourselves with each other, we compare ourselves in Christ. We are all equal. We are loved equally by our Father. We are all equally blessed and favored by Him. The Father rejoices and delights over you in the same way He rejoices and delights over me. He made us one with each other by making us one with Himself.

When we become conscious of this truth, there will be no more judging, jealousy, offense, or division among us. We have been invited into the circle of love. We are perfectly loved by our Heavenly Father. As we receive His perfect love, we'll be empowered to love each other with His perfect love, too.

Why did Jesus reveal the Father's character to you? (Verse 26)

_____

_____

_____

Jesus revealed the Father's character to us and will continue to reveal Him to us so that the love the Father bestowed on Him may also be felt in our hearts. We can

see from Jesus' prayer in John 17 that the Father has always planned for us to enjoy the same intimacy with Him that He and Jesus enjoy. It is the Father's desire for all of us to live in His love.

Follow Jesus example' of what it means to live in the Father's love by acknowledging the truth about your relationship with Him:

> *Father, I am in You and You are in me. You gave me Your glory and honor as Your love gift to me. Thank You for making me righteous in Christ Jesus! Father, I know You love me. You have loved me from the foundation of the world. Thank You for making me one with my brothers and sisters in Christ so that we can love each other with Your perfect love.*

Experience the level of intimacy the Father wants to have with you by establishing your heart in His love.

What have you learned today from Jesus' prayer about what it means to live in the Father's love?

_____

_____

_____

_____

How does it make your heart feel to realize that Jesus has given you the same honor and glory that the Father gave Him, by making you one with Himself?

_____

_____

_____

_____

Now that you realize that Jesus has made you equal with your brothers and sisters in Christ, how will it change the way you view yourself and the people God has placed in your life?

_____

_____

_____

_____

_____

WEEK 8

Perfect Love Casts Out All Fear

DAY 1:
Perfect Love Casts Out All Fear

DAY 2:
Living Fearlessly

DAY 3:
Cast Your Cares Upon Jesus

*[14]I bow my knees before the Father of our Lord Jesus Christ. [16]May He grant you out of the rich treasury of His glory to be strengthened and reinforced with mighty power in the inner man by the [Holy] Spirit [**Himself indwelling your innermost being and personality**]. [17]May Christ through your **faith** [actually] dwell (settle down, **abide**, make His permanent home) in your **hearts**! May you be rooted deep in love and founded securely on love, [18]That you may have the power and be strong to apprehend and grasp with all saints [God's devoted people, the experience of that love] what is the breadth and length and height and depth [of it]; [19][That you may really come] to know [practically, through experience for yourselves] the love of Christ which surpasses mere knowledge... that you might be **filled**... **unto all the fullness of God** [may have the richest measure of the divine Presence, and become a body wholly filled and flooded with God Himself]! [20]Now to Him Who, by (in consequence of) the [action of His] power that is at work within us, is able to [carry out His purpose and] do super abundantly, far over and above all that we [dare] ask or think [infinitely beyond our highest prayers, desires, thoughts, hopes or dreams] — [21]To Him be glory in the church and in Christ Jesus throughout all generations forever and ever. Amen (so it be)!*

EPHESIANS 3:14, 16-21 AMP

☙ Day 1 ❧
PERFECT LOVE CASTS OUT ALL FEAR

❧ Take time to pray before you begin. ❧

When you live loved, you live free from all fear. There are so many lies the devil throws at us in an attempt to fill our hearts with fear and worry. When we don't know and believe the love our Heavenly Father has for us, we live with a low-grade fear our whole lives. Because we're not quite sure of His love for us, we fear that something bad might happen in our lives. I used to live in fear. Fear of what people thought of me, fear about my finances, fear of sickness, concerns for my children, fear of failure, fear of harm, fear of talking in front of people. The root of all my fears was that I wasn't quite sure that God would really take care of the things that concerned me. I was unsure of His love for me.

Today, however, I am living loved and my heart is free from fear. Yes, there are times I am still tempted to be fearful, but when an anxious feeling comes to my heart, I turn to Jesus and ask Him to show me the truth that will set my heart free. He reminds me of His promise, and as I receive His love for me, my heart is filled with peace. His perfect love sets my heart free from all fear!

Read **1 John 4:16-19:**

¹⁶And we have known and believed the love that God has for us. God is love, and he who abides in love abides in God, and God in him. NKJV

¹⁷In this [union and communion with Him] love is brought to completion and attains perfection with us, that we may have confidence for the day of judgment [with assurance and boldness to face Him], because as He is, so are we in this world. AMP

¹⁸There is no fear in love; but perfect love casts out fear, because fear involves torment. But he who fears has not been made perfect in love. ¹⁹We love Him because He first loved us. NKJV

Verse 16 shows us that God is love and when we are mindful of His love, we are abiding in God and He is abiding in us.

How is God's love brought to completion in you? (Verse 17)

_____

_____

_____

Why can you live free from any fear of judgment and face your Heavenly Father with confidence? (Verse 17)

_____

_____

What will set you free from all fear? (Verse 18)

_____

If you have fear in your heart, what does it show? (Verse 18)

_____

Why do we love God?

_____

God's perfect love and fear cannot remain in your heart at the same time. They cannot coexist. His perfect love casts out all your fears. In the Amplified Bible verse 18 says, *(perfect) love turns fear out of doors and expels every trace of terror!* When you live with a low grade-fear it's because His love for you has not been perfected in your heart. You believe something about God or yourself that is not true.

When you are conscious of your union with Jesus (that you are one with Him) however, and you fellowship with Him daily, you'll live free from fear. Verse 17 says that it is through your union and communion with Him that love is brought to perfection in your heart. Your heart becomes established in His love when you live and abide in Him. You don't fear judgment. You come before your Heavenly Father with confidence because your heart is established in the truth that you are just like Jesus in this world. You are the righteousness of God in Him!

YOU ARE NO LONGER A FEARFUL SLAVE, BUT AN HEIR TO ALL OF GOD'S PROMISES

Romans 8:15-17: *[15]For [the Spirit which] you have now received [is] not a spirit of slavery **to put you once more in bondage to fear,** but you have received the Spirit of adoption... in... which we cry, Abba...Father! [16]The Spirit Himself... testifies together with our spirit, [assuring us] that we are children of God. [17]And if we are [His] children, then we are [His] heirs also; heirs of God and fellow heirs with Christ."* AMP

What have you received through your union with Jesus?

_____

_____

_____

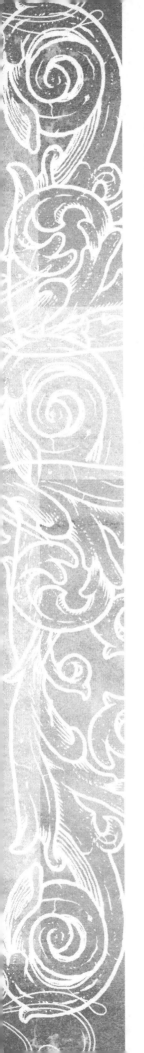

Often when fear comes at my heart, the Holy Spirit will remind me that I am not a fearful slave. Jesus set me free from the bondage of fear by making me a daughter of God. I can cry, "Father, I know You love me. I don't have to be afraid. I am an heir to all of Your promises because of my union with Jesus." In my union and communion with Him, His love is brought to perfection in my soul!

GOD'S PERFECT LOVE IS REVEALED IN JESUS

Romans 8:39: *Whether we are high above the sky or in the deepest ocean, nothing in all creation will ever be able to separate us from **the love of God that is revealed in Christ Jesus our Lord.** NLT[1]*

God's perfect love for us is revealed in the promises we have been given in Jesus. Each treasure we have in Christ is a revelation of His love.

GOD'S PROMISES ARE "YES" AND "AMEN" IN CHRIST JESUS

2 Corinthians 1:19-20: *[19]For Jesus Christ, the Son of God, does not waver between "Yes" and "No." He is the one whom Silas, Timothy, and I preached to you, and as God's ultimate "Yes," he always does what he says. [20] For all of God's promises have been fulfilled in Christ with a resounding "Yes!" And through Christ, our "Amen" (which means "Yes") ascends to God for his glory. NLT[2]*

[20]For no matter how many promises God has made, they are "Yes" in Christ. And so through him the "Amen" is spoken by us to the glory of God. NIV

What does God say concerning all of His promises to you in Christ?

_____

_____

BECAUSE YOU ARE IN CHRIST JESUS, YOUR HEAVENLY FATHER SAYS "YES!" TO ALL OF HIS PROMISES:

YES! *You are the righteousness of God in Christ Jesus!* 2 Corinthians 5:21

YES! *I have given My angels charge over you to protect you in all your ways!* Psalm 91

YES! *You are highly favored and abundantly blessed!* Psalm 5:11,12; 2 Corinthians 9:8

YES! *You are qualified and anointed to share the Good News!* 2 Corinthians 3:4-6

YES! *I accept and approve of you!* Ephesians 1:6

YES! *You are holy and without fault in My sight!* Ephesians 1:4

YES! *I create in you the desire and the power to do what pleases Me!* Philippians 2:13

YES! *I set you free from all sin!* Romans 6:11-14

YES! *You are forgiven. I don't even remember your sins!* Hebrews 8:12

YES! *You are free from all condemnation and guilt!* Romans 8:1

YES! *My plan is to prosper you and give you hope for your future!* Jeremiah 29:11

YES! *Your children are mighty and blessed upon the earth!* Psalm 112:2

YES! *I will fulfill the desires of your heart!* Psalm 37:4

YES! *By My stripes you are healed!* Isaiah 53:5

YES! *During times of famine, you will have more than enough!* Psalm 37:17-19

YES! *I will teach your children and give them great peace!* Isaiah 54:13

YES! *I will deliver you from all your troubles!* Psalm 34:19

YES! *You hear my voice and are led by My Spirit!* Romans 8:14

YES! *You are equipped with everything you need to carry out My will!* Hebrews 13:20,21

YES! *You are complete in Christ. You lack nothing!* Colossians 2:10

Which of these promises particularly ministered to your heart today?

_____

_____

_____

What do each of these promises in Christ reveal about your
Heavenly Father's heart toward you?
HE LOVES YOU!

How does Jesus want you to respond to each one of these promises? 2 Corinthians 1:20

_____

_____

Read back over each promise again and let them soak deep within your heart. Take a moment to ponder on the significance of your union with Christ. It's because you are one with Jesus that God says, "Yes!" to His promises in your life. Because you are in Christ Jesus, you can boldly say, "Amen, Lord! I know You love me! Your promises are true in my life!"

My heart is free from all fear when I agree with the One Who loves me. I remember one such occasion when fear tried to grip my heart. It was 2001 and the economy was hit hard and people began losing their jobs. My husband came home one day from work to tell me he would be losing his job as well. I remember the fear that tried to enter my heart as this thought came to my mind, *What are we going to do?*

I picked up my Bible from my night-stand and went downstairs to talk with my

Heavenly Father. I remember saying, "Heavenly Father, help me to trust You in this situation." As the Holy Spirit began to remind me of the promises I have in Jesus, I responded by saying, "Father, I know You love me because You said Your plan is to prosper us and to give us hope and a future (Jeremiah 29:11). I know You love me because You promised to cause all grace to abound toward us so that we would have more than enough to meet all our needs (2 Corinthians 9:8-11). I know You love me, Father, because You said that You take care of the birds in the air and You promised to take care of us" (Matthew 6:25-33).

My heart was established in the truth that my Heavenly Father says "Yes" to all of His promises in my life because I am in Christ Jesus. All I had to do was receive them by saying, "Amen! Lord, what you say about me is true!" Through my union and communion with Him, His love was brought to completion within my heart. His perfect love cast out all my fears!

Over the next few months, my husband started His own business and his income doubled. I experienced God's promise of peace and prosperity simply by agreeing with the One Who loves me.

Read **2 Peter 1:3,4:** *3As we know Jesus better, his divine power gives us everything we need for living a godly life. He has called us to receive His own glory and goodness. NLT [1]*

4Through these he has given us his very great and precious promises, so that through them you may participate in the divine nature and escape the corruption in the world caused by evil desires. NIV

What has God's divine power given to you? What has he called you to receive? (Verse 3)

_____

_____

_____

Why did God give you His great and precious promises? (Verse 4)

_____

_____

_____

Your Heavenly Father has given you everything you need to live a life free from fear. He has called you to receive His glory and goodness. God has given you His great and precious promises so you can escape the devil's plan of fear and bondage and partake of God's divine nature.

The next time the devil tempts you to worry or be fearful, turn your heart to the Father and talk to Him about His great love for you. Remember it is through your union and communion with Him that His love is brought to perfection in your heart.

You can confidently come before Him and say, "Father, I know You love me because of the promise You've given me in Jesus." When you agree with the Father's promise to you, you'll live fearless, confident and secure in Jesus, and your life will glorify God. His perfect love will cast out all your fears!

What did you learn today about how living loved sets you free from fear? How will you apply it in your life?

_____

_____

_____

_____

_____

_____

_____

_____

_____

ꙮ Day 2 ꙮ
LIVING FEARLESSLY

꙳ Take time to pray before you begin. ꙳

Jesus lived a fearless life here on the earth. Living fearlessly however, does not mean that you never feel fear in your heart. What it does mean is that when you're tempted to worry about something, you look to Jesus and receive His grace to empower you to trust Him instead. The Bible says that Jesus was tempted in every way that we are. He understands what if feels like to be tempted to be afraid, but He also showed us that the way to freedom is through union and communion with the Father. He too, went to the throne of grace to receive the strength He needed to overcome. We can see His example to us very clearly in **Mark 14:32-55** AMP:

> *³²Then they went to a place called Gethsemane, and He said to His disciples, Sit down here while I pray. ³³And He took with Him Peter and James and John, and began to be struck with terror and amazement and deeply troubled and depressed. ³⁴And He said to them, My soul is exceedingly sad (overwhelmed with grief) so that it almost kills Me! Remain here and keep awake and be watching.*

What negative emotions did Jesus feel in his soul?

_____

_____

_____

Jesus was tempted to be afraid. The Scriptures say His heart was stricken with terror. Fear gripped His heart. He felt depressed and deeply troubled. Somehow realizing that Jesus felt the same way I feel at times, encourages me and endears Him to my heart. Have you ever shared your heart with a good friend and were comforted to know that they had felt the same way that you did? Jesus is your best friend and He can relate to the negative emotions your heart feels because He was tempted in every way that you are. He sympathizes with you. He truly understands what it feels like to be afraid to the point of sweating great drops of blood. **Luke 22:44** says, *And being in an agony he prayed more earnestly: and his sweat was as it were great drops of blood falling down to the ground. KJV*

JESUS FELT AGONY FROM THE FEAR THAT GRIPPED HIS HEART, BUT HIS HEART WAS SET FREE THROUGH HIS UNION AND COMMUNION WITH HIS FATHER

> *³⁵And going a little farther, He fell on the ground and kept praying that if it were possible the [fatal] hour might pass from Him. ³⁶And He was saying, Abba,*

[which means] Father, everything is possible for You. Take away this cup from Me; yet not what I will, but what You [will].

Jesus shared His fear with His Father. He was honest with Him about how He felt. Then He said, *"Abba Father, not what I will, but what you will."* He acknowledged His fear, but was willing to trust His Father completely because He knew His Father loved Him.

³⁷And He came back and found them sleeping, and He said to Peter, Simon, are you asleep? Have you not the strength to keep awake and watch [with Me for] one hour?

If Jesus was tempted in every way that you are, how do you think Jesus felt when He realized that His friends had let Him down?

---

³⁸Keep awake and watch and pray [constantly], that you may not enter into temptation; the spirit indeed is willing, but the flesh is weak.

What did Jesus say would empower us to overcome every temptation?

Again we see Jesus sharing the secret to living a life free from sin. Prayer is not something we do just before we eat or for ten minutes in the morning during our devotional time. Prayer is a lifestyle of constant fellowship with the Father and the Son. It's not a religious duty, but an intimate relationship with the One Who loves us and meets all the needs of our heart. When we live in intimacy with Jesus, inviting Him into every facet of our hearts — by sharing our fears, frustrations, doubts, and struggles with Him — He empowers us with His grace. In our weakness, He makes us strong (2 Corinthians 12:9).

³⁹He went away again and prayed, saying the same words. ⁴⁰And again He came back and found them sleeping, for their eyes were very heavy; and they did not know what answer to give Him. ⁴¹And He came back a third time and said to them, Are you still sleeping and resting? It is enough [of that]! The hour has come. The Son of Man is betrayed into the hands of sinful men (men whose way or nature is to act in opposition to God). ⁴²Get up, let us be going! See, My betrayer is at hand! ⁴³And at once, while He was still speaking, Judas came, one of the Twelve [apostles], and with him a crowd of men with swords and clubs, [who came] from the chief priests and the scribes and the elders [of the Sanhedrin]. ⁴⁴Now the betrayer had given them a signal, saying, The One I shall kiss is [the

Man]; seize Him and lead [Him] away safely [so as to prevent His escape]. 45And when he came, he went up to Jesus immediately and said, Master! Master! and he embraced Him and kissed Him fervently. 46And they threw their hands on Him and arrested Him. 47But one of the bystanders drew his sword and struck the bond servant of the high priest and cut off his ear. 48And Jesus said to them, Have you come out with swords and clubs as [you would] against a robber to capture Me? 49I was with you daily in the temple [porches and courts] teaching, and you did not seize Me; but [this has happened] that the Scriptures might be fulfilled. AMP

JESUS KNEW WHERE TO GO WHEN HE WAS TEMPTED

He ran to the Father who loved Him. He knew that it was through His union and communion with His Father that He would receive the strength He needed to carry out the Father's plan for His life. He went into the garden of Gethsemane feeling fearful and afraid, but He came out empowered by the Holy Spirit. He faced His accusers fearlessly and fulfilled the Father's plan for His life because His heart was filled with the Father's love.

> **Hebrews 12:2** says: *Looking away [from all that will distract] to Jesus, Who is the Leader and the Source of our faith [giving the first incentive for our belief] and is also its Finisher [bringing it to maturity and perfection]. He, for the joy [of obtaining the prize] that was set before Him, endured the cross, despising and ignoring the shame, and is now seated at the right hand of the throne of God. AMP*

The Bible says that for the joy of obtaining the prize that was set before Him, Jesus endured the cross. His prize was being seated in the highest place of honor at the right hand of the Father and making it possible for us to be seated in Him. He knew His Father would fulfill the desire of His heart because of His great love.

> In **John 17:24** Jesus prayed: *"I desire that they also whom You have entrusted to Me [as Your gift to Me] may be with Me where I am, so that they may see My glory, which You have given Me [Your love gift to Me]; for You loved Me before the foundation of the world." AMP*

Wow! It was the desire of Jesus' heart that we would sit with Him in the highest place of honor. What love He has demonstrated toward us to go through such agony and grief in order to give us such a priceless gift. He made it possible for all of us to live free from fear by bringing us into that same intimate relationship with Him and the Father.

Jesus went to the cross fearlessly because He knew His Father's promise, and He was secure in His Father's love. In **John 17:24** He said, *"Father… You have loved me before the foundation of the world."* I often find myself following Jesus' example when

I am tempted with fear and worry. I softly pray, *"Father, I know You love me because of the promises You've given me in Christ. I can rest in your great love!"*

You, too, can live free from fear by living in the same relationship with the Father that Jesus did. Take the fears, frustrations, worries, concerns, and struggles of your heart to the Father. Live conscious of His love for you. Live in constant union and communion with Him and you too, will be empowered by the Holy Spirit to live fearlessly in this world.

What did you learn from watching Jesus interact with His Father during the moment of His greatest temptation?

_____

_____

_____

_____

_____

How can you follow His example and live loved and live free?

_____

_____

_____

_____

_____

_____

_____

_____

_____

_____

Day 3
CAST YOUR CARES UPON JESUS

Take time to pray before you begin.

There are so many things in this world that the devil uses to tempt us to worry. Our finances, our health, our children, the economy, our reputation, and our future are just a few of the things that can cause us concern. The devil knows that if we live in fear and worry, we won't be able to experience all that Jesus died to give us. Even though we're sons and daughters of the King, we'll live like fearful slaves.

Jesus came so that you could reign in this life like a king (Romans 5:17). He made it possible for you to live free from all worry and fear. Jesus loves you so much that He told you in His word to bring every care and concern of your heart to Him.

Read **1 Peter 5:7**: *Casting the whole of your care [all your anxieties, all your worries, all your concerns, once and for all] on Him, for He cares for you affectionately and cares about you watchfully. AMP*

Why can you bring every worry and concern of your heart to Jesus?

_____

_____

WHAT DOES IT MEAN TO CAST YOUR CARES UPON JESUS?

When you cast your cares upon Jesus, you give your cares to Him in prayer and you receive His promise into your heart. You share your concerns with Him and then begin to think upon what He says about your situation.

WHAT ARE SOME THINGS WE ARE TEMPTED TO WORRY ABOUT?

FEARS	GOD'S PROMISES
Finances	2 Corinthians 9:8; Matthew 6:25-33
Our children	Isaiah 54:13; Psalm 112:1-2; Proverbs 11:21
What others think of us	Psalm 139:14-18; Ephesians 1:4
Economy	Psalm 37:18-19
Protection	Psalm 91
Health	Proverbs 4:20-22
Decisions	Proverbs 16:3; Proverbs 3:5-6
Fear of failure	Psalm 1:1-3
Trials of life	Psalm 34:17-19

Recently, I was tempted to worry about a decision I needed to make. I simply took this concern to the Lord in prayer and said, "Lord, I thank You that You promised to cause my thoughts to be agreeable to Your will so that my plans will prosper and succeed (Proverbs 16:3). I know You love me, Lord. You lead me by Your Spirit." My heart was filled with peace as I thought upon His promise to me, and I was able to make the decision with perfect peace in my heart.

> Read **Philippians 4:6-9**: *⁶Don't worry about anything; instead, pray about everything. Tell God what you need, and thank him for all he has done. ⁷Then you will experience God's peace, which exceeds anything we can understand. His peace will guard your hearts and minds as you live in Christ Jesus. ⁸And now, dear brothers and sisters, one final thing. Fix your thoughts on what is true, and honorable, and right, and pure, and lovely, and admirable. Think about things that are excellent and worthy of praise. ⁹Keep putting into practice all you learned and received from me—everything you heard from me and saw me doing. Then the God of peace will be with you. NLT²*

What does verse 6 tell you to do?

_____

_____

_____

What will you experience when you live in Jesus? (Verse 7)

_____

_____

What does Jesus want you to fill your mind with? (Verse 8)

_____

_____

_____

Isaiah 26:3 says: *You keep in perfect peace all who trust in you, all **whose thoughts are fixed on you.** NLT²*

Read **John 16:33**: *I have told you these things so that in Me you may have [perfect] peace and confidence. In the world you will have tribulation and trials and distress and frustration; but be of good cheer [take courage; be confident; certain, undaunted]! For I have overcome the world. [I have deprived it of power to harm you and have conquered it for you.] AMP*

Why did Jesus speak His words of love to you?

_____

_____

What did He say you would experience in this world?

_____

_____

Why can you be confident and joyful no matter what difficult situation you may face?

_____

_____

Jesus speaks His promises to your heart so that you can have perfect peace and confidence in this world. There is no trial or temptation that you can face in this life that Jesus has not already overcome for you. He made you more than a conqueror through your union with Him. You can be joyful and confident because you are in Christ Jesus and every promise of God is *yes* and **amen** in your life. His promises cover every fear and concern of your heart. He has given you a promise of victory for every problem you could ever face in this world. He already won the victory for you so all you need to do is rest in Him with a thankful heart.

Receive His Promises With a Thankful Heart

Read **1 Thessalonians 5:16-18:** *Be happy [in your faith] and rejoice and be glad-hearted continually....Be unceasing in prayer....Thank [God] in everything [no matter what the circumstances may be, be thankful and give thanks], for this is the will of God for you [who are] in Christ Jesus. AMP*

What is God's will for you in Christ?

_____

_____

Read **Colossians 2:7:** *Let your roots grow down into him, and let your lives be built on him. Then your faith will grow strong in the truth you were taught, and you will overflow with thankfulness. NLT²*

Psalm 119:162 says: *I rejoice in your word like one who discovers a great treasure. NLT²*

The New Century Version of **Psalm 119:162** says: *I am as happy over your promises as if I had found a great treasure.*

This verse reminds me of the endless treasures available to us in Christ Jesus. What joy we can live in when we keep our mind on the promises we have in Him. Colossians 2:7 says that when your roots grow down into Jesus, your faith will grow strong in the truth, and your heart will overflow with thanksgiving. This is the kind of life that the Father wants you and me to live. He wants us to be happy in Jesus and receive His promises with a thankful heart. The Father created us to live in His love.

Psalm 50:23 says: *He who brings an offering of praise and thanksgiving honors and glorifies Me…to him I will demonstrate the salvation of God. AMP*

According to *Lexical Aid to the New Testament*, the word *salvation* in this verse "is inclusive of all the blessings of God." It includes every promise Jesus purchased for you. When you live in Jesus with a thankful heart, you'll experience the salvation of God in every area of your life.

Read **Hebrews 6:17-19:** *[17] God also bound Himself with an oath, so that those who received the promise could be perfectly sure that he would never change his mind. [18] So God has given us both his promise and his oath. These two things are unchangeable because it is impossible for God to lie. Therefore, we who have fled to him for refuge can take new courage, for we can hold on to his promise with confidence. [19] This confidence is like a strong and trustworthy anchor for our souls. NLT[1]*

Why can you hold onto God's promise with confidence? (Verse 18)

_____

What is our confidence in God's promise like? (19)

_____

_____

We all need an anchor for our soul when we are faced with difficult situations in our lives. The promises you have in Jesus are like a strong and trustworthy anchor for your soul. You can hold onto God's promise with confidence because it is impossible for God to lie. He is completely trustworthy! You can run to your Heavenly Father for refuge whenever you're being tempted to worry or fear and simply ask Him, "Father, what do You say about this situation in my life?" He will remind you of who you are in Jesus and the promise you have in Him. He will give you an anchor for your soul. Through your union and communion with Him His love will be perfected in your heart. You will live free from all fear as you live in His love.

Have you been tempted to worry or fear about something in your life?

_____

_____

_____

_____

_____

_____

_____

Ask the Father right now what He says about your situation. Write the promise you have in Jesus that He speaks to your heart on the lines below. What is the anchor for your soul?

_____

_____

_____

_____

_____

_____

_____

_____

_____

_____

Share with another brother or sister in Christ this treasure you have in Jesus. There's no greater joy than to live in the love of Jesus and share His love with others.

WEEK 9

A Place of Rest

DAY 1:
A Life Lived in Trust

DAY 2:
Come to Jesus to Find Rest

DAY 3:
Grace: The Power to Believe

[14]*I bow my knees before the Father of our Lord Jesus Christ.* [16]*May He grant you out of the rich treasury of His glory to be strengthened and reinforced with mighty power in the inner man by the Holy Spirit (Himself indwelling your innermost being and personality).* [17]*May Christ through your faith [actually] dwell (settle down, abide, make His permanent home) in your hearts! May you be rooted deep in love and founded securely on love,* [18]*That you may have the power and be strong to apprehend and grasp with all saints [God's devoted people, the experience of that love] what is the breadth and length and height and depth [of it];* [19][*That you may really come] to know [practically, through experience for yourselves] the love of Christ which surpasses mere knowledge... that you might be filled... [with] the fullness of God [may have the richest measure of the divine Presence, and become a body wholly filled and flooded with God Himself]!* [20]*Now to Him Who, by (in consequence of) the [action of His] power that is at work within us, is able to [carry out His purpose and] do super abundantly, far over and above all that we dare ask or think [infinitely beyond our highest prayers, desires, thoughts, hopes or dreams] —* [21]*To Him be glory in the church and in Christ Jesus throughout all generations forever and ever. Amen (so be it)!*

EPHESIANS 3:14-21 AMP

❧ Day 1 ❧

A LIFE LIVED IN TRUST

❧ Take time to pray before you begin. ❧

God has promised His children a place of rest. It is a place where our hearts are free from fear and insecurity. When we live loved by Him we enter into His rest because we trust Him completely. Yet so many of God's children never really experience this promise of rest; so many continue to live with condemnation, shame, and fear in their hearts even after they've heard the Good News of God's love and grace. One day I asked, "Lord, what keeps many of your children from really entering into Your rest and experiencing your promises in their lives?" What keeps them from experiencing the perfect and constant peace that you've promised them? Why is it that so many live with wounded hearts when you've promised to make them whole? In response to my questions, the Holy Spirit led me to the following passage of Scripture.

> Read **Jeremiah 15:18-21:** *¹⁸Why is my pain perpetual and my wound incurable, refusing to be healed? Will you indeed be to me like a deceitful brook, like waters that fail and are uncertain? ¹⁹Therefore thus says the Lord [to Jeremiah]: If you return [and give up this mistaken tone of distrust and despair], then I will give you again a settled place of quiet and safety, and you will be My minister; and if you separate the precious from the vile [cleansing your own heart from unworthy and unwarranted suspicions concerning God's faithfulness], you shall be My mouthpiece... ²⁰And I will make you to this people a fortified, bronze wall; they will fight against you, but they will not prevail over you, for I am with you to save and deliver you, says the Lord. ²¹And I will deliver you out of the hands of the wicked, and I will redeem you. AMP*

What were the questions that Jeremiah had within his heart? (Verse 18)

_____

_____

How did God respond to Jeremiah? What did He tell Jeremiah to do so that he could find rest for his soul? (Verse 19)

_____

What did God promise Jeremiah if he would let go of his suspicions concerning God's faithfulness and choose to trust Him completely? (Verse 20-21)

_____

_____

Jeremiah was facing a very dark time in his life. It seemed as though nothing was going the way he hoped. He felt depression and disappointment within his soul and could not seem to find peace in his heart. So he asked this question, "Lord, why is my pain perpetual? Why is my heart not healed? Have You lied to me Lord? Are Your promises really true? Have You failed me?" His heart was questioning God's faithfulness?

Have you ever been in a place in your life where you questioned God's promises? When your circumstances didn't seem to be changing and you felt like God was far away? Has your heart ever asked these questions, *Lord, where are You?* or *Can I really trust You?*

You may have even heard the Good News that you are complete in Christ and that all of His promises to you are *Yes* and *Amen*, but still, your heart is saying, *I feel so incomplete. I lack in so many ways. It just sounds too good to be true?* The lies are somehow easier to believe because that is how your heart feels.

I remember back to a time when I used to question God's promises. My own personal experiences of failure and other people's negative experiences made me question the validity of God's Word. "Lord, where are you?" I would ask. "Do you even hear my prayers? Have you failed me? Can I really trust you? Is what you say about me really true?" Without my awareness, my mistaken tone of distrust was creating perpetual pain in my heart, just like Jeremiah's. My heart could not be healed as long as I questioned God's faithfulness.

> *Give up this mistaken tone of distrust and despair, then I will give you a place of rest and safety.*

BUT WHAT IS THE SOLUTION TO THIS PERPETUAL PAIN?

The same answer God gave to Jeremiah is the one He gives to you and me: *If you'll return and give up this mistaken tone of distrust and despair then I will give you a place of rest and safety, and you will be my minister. If you'll separate the precious — the Truth; from the vile: the lies concerning my faithfulness — then you will stand strong in faith, and I will save and deliver you, says the Lord.*

Through these verses it became very clear to me that the reason many of God's children never experience His promise of rest is because they won't let go of their questions concerning God's faithfulness. Instead of trusting Him and receiving the truth that will set their heart free, they hold onto the lies that have kept them in bondage their whole lives. The darkest moments of my life have been when my heart questioned the Good News. *Is what God says about me really true? Are His promises really true? It just doesn't seem to be working for me. Can I really trust God and His love for me?* There's no greater pain in the heart of a believer than to carry in your heart a tone of distrust and unwarranted suspicions about God's faithfulness.

The devil often uses the negative circumstances in our lives to cause us to question

God's love and faithfulness: a negative childhood experience, a divorce or bankruptcy, the loss of a child or business. He likes to taunt us with our failures, making us feel ashamed of our unanswered prayers, or unchanging negative circumstances. Every one of us has experienced disappointments in life. But none of these things change the truth: God's word is true, He is faithful, and He is completely trustworthy!

> Read **Romans 8:35-37**: *[35] Can anything ever separate us from Christ's love? Does it mean he no longer loves us if we have trouble or calamity, or are persecuted, or hungry, or destitute, or in danger, or threatened with death? [36] (As the Scriptures say, "For your sake we are killed every day; we are being slaughtered like sheep.") [37] No, despite all these things, overwhelming victory is ours through Christ, who loved us.* NLT[2]

What questions did the Apostle Paul have about God's love? (Verse 35)

_____

_____

_____

What conclusion did he come to in his heart? What did he choose to believe? (Verse 37)

_____

_____

I love how the Apostle Paul asks a question that we have all wondered in our own hearts, and then he confidently answers himself with the truth. He established his heart in the truth of God's love and made a decision to trust Him even in the midst of difficult circumstances.

When my heart begins to question God's faithfulness because of something I don't understand, the Holy Spirit always reminds me of one of my favorite Scriptures, which always brings peace to my heart:

> **Proverbs 3:5-6**: *[5] Trust in the LORD with all your heart and lean not on your own understanding; [6] in all your ways acknowledge him, and he will make your paths straight.* NIV

When I make the choice in my heart to trust the Lord completely, that is when I find true peace in my soul. When I let go of the lies my heart is tempted to believe and I pray, "Heavenly Father, I choose to trust You! No matter how I feel or what I see, I trust what You say is true," that's when I enter into that place of rest and experience God's delivering power in my life.

One of the darkest times in my life happened when my husband was going through a deep depression. The devil had attacked his mind and he became deeply depressed. I had been praying for months that God would deliver him, but nothing seemed to be changing. Most days I kept my eyes on Jesus, finding strength and hope in the promises I had in Him.

One particular day after my husband had been battling this for months and it didn't look like my prayers were working at all, the devil came and attacked my mind with his lies. The enemy began throwing his fiery darts at my heart and his lies began to fill my thoughts. I began to question God's faithfulness. I even questioned whether the Bible was really true. I even had this lie pass through my thoughts, *Are you sure there is even a God at all?* Darkness enveloped me as I pondered these suspicions about God and His faithfulness. My heart was filled with perpetual pain and I felt depressed and hopeless.

In quietness and in [trusting] confidence shall be your strength

I remember turning to Jesus and asking for His grace to continue to trust Him. In response to my prayer the Holy Spirit reminded me of God's word in **Isaiah 30:15:** *For thus said the Lord God, the Holy One of Israel: In returning [to Me] and resting [in] Me you shall be saved; in quietness and in [trusting] confidence shall be your strength.* AMP

I realized I had a choice to make within my own heart — I could surrender these lies to the truth of my Heavenly Father's love and faithfulness and experience His strength and peace in my soul, or I could receive these lies as my truth and live in perpetual pain. Again the Holy Spirit spoke to my heart by reminding me of **Hebrews 10:35-36,** *³⁵Do not, therefore, fling away your fearless confidence, for it carries a great and glorious compensation of reward. ³⁶For you have need of steadfast patience and endurance, so that you may perform and fully accomplish the will of God, and thus receive and carry away [and enjoy to the full] what is promised.* AMP

That day I prayed, "Father, I choose to trust You! I know you love me and You are faithful!" When I separated the precious from the vile and gave up my suspicions of God's faithfulness, I found quietness and rest within my soul. In returning to Him and trusting Him with all my heart I found new strength. In the weeks to come I saw God deliver my husband from depression and fill his heart with joy once again. I experienced the delivering power of God and enjoyed to the full what He had promised.

By God's grace, every day and in every situation, I continue to choose to trust the Father's love and promises to me in Christ. That is where true freedom and rest in Christ is found.

You and I can live free from perpetual pain in our hearts caused by questioning the truth of what Jesus really accomplished on the cross for us. If you want to live in the place of rest that God has promised you in Christ, give up any suspicions in your heart concerning God's love and faithfulness. Let go of the lies you've believed

about God or yourself and acknowledge your choice to trust Him completely. **1 John 4:16** says, *We know how much God loves us and we have put our trust in His love.* NLT² It's when we come to Jesus and surrender all our doubts and fears to Him that we will truly live in a place of rest and experience His salvation in every area of our lives. It is then that we will truly live loved and live free!

Have you ever had suspicions of God's faithfulness within your heart? Have you ever questioned His love and promises to you? During those moments, what has this questioning produced in your heart?

_____

_____

_____

How can you live in a place of rest in Christ and experience God's power in your heart and life?

_____

_____

_____

_____

_____

_____

_____

_____

_____

❦ Day 2 ❦
COME TO JESUS TO FIND REST

"Are you tired? Worn out? Burned out on religion? Come to me. Get away with me and you'll recover your life. I'll show you how to take a real rest. Walk with me and work with me—watch how I do it. Learn the unforced rhythms of grace. I won't lay anything heavy or ill-fitting on you. Keep company with me and you'll learn to live freely and lightly."

MATTHEW 11:28-30 MSG

❧ Take time to pray before you begin. ❧

In these verses Jesus is inviting you to come and get away with Him and recover your life. He says He'll teach you how to truly rest, by trusting Him with all your heart. As you walk in intimacy with Jesus, you'll learn to live in His grace; to live freely and lightly. What a wonderful promise we have in Jesus!

Jesus demonstrated a heart that fully trusted in the love of His Father when He prayed in Mark 14:36, *"Father... not what I will, but what You will,"* NKJV and in Luke 23:46, *"Father, I entrust my spirit into your hands."* NLT² During the most difficult moments of His life, He surrendered His opinions, and His way to the Father's. He knew that no matter how His heart felt at that moment, His Father was right and He could trust in His love!

When we make the daily decision to trust our Heavenly Father's love and opinion of us, we'll find true peace in our hearts. When we pray like Jesus, "Father, I entrust my whole life to You. I trust what You say about me and know you have a good plan for my life," that's when we will find true rest for our souls. Remember, your Heavenly Father loves you and His opinion of you is very good! His plan is to prosper you and give you a hope and a future. He is trustworthy and you can rest in Him.

Read **Hebrews 4:1-13**: *¹Therefore, while the promise of entering His rest still holds and is offered [today], let us be afraid [to distrust it], lest any of you should think he has come too late and has come short of [reaching] it. AMP*

What promise is revealed in this verse?

_____

_____

What did he say to be afraid of?

_____

_____

_____

This Scripture tells us to be afraid to distrust the promise of entering God's rest. The only true place of security in this world is in this place of rest that the Father has provided for us in Christ. When we trust the One Who loves us, we live safely and securely in His love.

Rest means:

- Freedom from anything that tires, troubles, or disturbs you
- To be free from care, worry, fear, and anxiety
- To have peace
- To trust and rely upon someone *(Thorndike Dictionary)*

When you've entered this promise of rest in Christ, you live free from anything that tires, troubles or disturbs you. You live free from stress, worry, and fear. You experience perfect and constant peace as you trust and rely upon Jesus.

> **Hebrews 4:2-3** says: *²For indeed we have had the glad tidings [Gospel of God] proclaimed to us just as truly as they [the Israelites of old did when the good news of deliverance from bondage came to them]; but the message they heard did not benefit them, because it was not mixed with faith (with the leaning of the entire personality on God in absolute trust and confidence in His power, wisdom, and goodness) by those who heard it; neither were they united in faith with the ones [Joshua and Caleb] who heard (did believe). ³For we who have believed (adhered to and trusted in and relied on God) do enter that rest. AMP*

We have had the Good News of the treasures available in Christ proclaimed to us just as the children of Israel did when the Good News of deliverance came to them; but God's promises didn't benefit them because they didn't believe what God said about them was true.

God promised to deliver the Israelites and bring them into a land of abundance, where all their needs would be met and they would lack nothing. But because they had unwarranted suspicions of God's faithfulness in their hearts, they refused to trust Him. They chose instead to trust in their own ability and opinion of themselves. They saw themselves as grasshoppers instead of children of the King and it cost them dearly. Instead of enjoying the life of abundance that God had promised them, they died in the wilderness (Hebrews 3:15-19).

Joshua and Caleb on the other hand, responded differently to the Good News. They chose to believe what God said about them and fully trust in His power, wisdom, and goodness. They even tried to encourage the others to view themselves the way God saw them. They said "believe what God says about you and He will bring you into this place of abundance just like He promised." But the others refused to give up the lies they had chosen to believe about themselves, and God. As a result, they gave up their inheritance. Yet Joshua and Caleb trusted in God's love and faithfulness, and as a result, they and their children, enjoyed to the full all that God had promised them.

The Good News is that you have been made the righteousness of God in Christ Jesus

All the promises and treasures in Christ are "Yes" and "Amen" in your life because of Jesus. You are no longer a fearful slave trying to earn God's blessing, but you are a son or daughter of the King and everything the Father has belongs to you. Jesus set you free from condemnation and shame. Your old sinful self was crucified with Christ and sin has lost its power in your life. Jesus gave you His honor and glory by making you one with Himself. You sit in the highest place of honor in Christ. Your Heavenly Father honors you by declaring you righteous, abundantly blessed, highly favored, and an heir to all His promised blessings because of your faith in Jesus. You are complete in Jesus. You lack nothing! Your Heavenly Father says you're very, very good and He rejoices over you with ecstatic delight. When you believe this Good News you enter into the promise of rest and enjoy your inheritance as a son or daughter of the King.

There have been times in my life that I've responded to the Good News like the children of Israel did, and believed the lie that *I am not who God says I am*. This only served to cause perpetual pain in my heart and kept me in bondage to worry, insecurity, and sin. But there have been other times I've responded just like Joshua and Caleb, and boldly declared, "I am who my Father says I am in Jesus! I am the righteousness of God in Christ. I am loved and abundantly blessed because of Jesus!" When my heart agrees with the One Who loves me, I enter into His promise of rest, and partake of the treasures available to me in Jesus!

> Read **Hebrews 4:4-7:** *⁴For in a certain place He has said this about the seventh day: And God rested on the seventh day from all His works. ⁵And [they forfeited their part in it, for] in this [passage] He said, They shall not enter My rest. ⁶Seeing then that the promise remains over [from past times] for some to enter that rest, and that those who formerly were given the good news about it and the opportunity, failed to appropriate it and did not enter because of disobedience, ⁷Again He sets a definite day, [a new] Today, [and gives another opportunity of securing that rest] saying through David after so long a time in the words already quoted, Today, if you would hear His voice and when you hear it, do not harden your hearts. AMP*

The children of Israel did not enter God's rest and forfeited their inheritance because they chose not to believe God. They held on to their own opinion and trusted in themselves. These verses warn us not to follow their example.

When you hear the Good News of who you are in Jesus, what does verse 7 tell you not to do?

_____

Every day our Heavenly Father gives us the choice to trust Him or not to trust Him. The promise of entering His rest is new every morning! Today when you hear Him speak to your heart and remind you of who you truly are in Jesus, don't harden your heart. Don't refuse the freedom He offers by holding on to the lies of the enemy and taking on your own opinion of yourself.

Read **Hebrews 4:8-12**: *⁸[This mention of a rest was not a reference to their entering into Canaan.] For if Joshua had given them rest, He [God] would not speak afterward about another day. ⁹So then, there is still awaiting a full and complete Sabbath-rest reserved for the [true] people of God; ¹⁰For he who has once entered [God's] rest also has ceased from [the weariness and pain] of human labors, just as God rested from those labors peculiarly His own ¹¹ Let us therefore be zealous and exert ourselves and strive diligently to enter that rest [of God, to know and experience it for ourselves], that no one may fail or perish by same kind of unbelief and disobedience [into which those in the wilderness fell].¹² For the word that God speaks is alive and full of power [making it active, operative, energizing, and effective].* AMP

Hebrews 4:12-13 in the Message Bible: *¹²God means what he says. What he says goes. His powerful Word is sharp as a surgeon's scalpel, cutting through everything, whether doubt or defense, laying us open to listen and obey. ¹³Nothing and no one is impervious to God's Word. We can't get away from it—no matter what.*"

What does Hebrews 4:9 assure you of?

_____

When you enter God's rest what do you cease to do? (Verse 10)

_____

Look at verse 12 in the Amplified Bible and verses 12-13 in the Message. What do these verses say about God's Word?

_____

_____

_____

God means what He says, and what He says is the absolute truth and final authority in your life. His word is alive and full of power and you can trust what He says about you! God has prepared a complete and total Sabbath rest for you and me. It is a place where we cease to try to be who God has already made us in Christ.

It is a place where we cease to try to earn something we already have in Him. We rest in the finished work of Jesus! He's already taken care of everything that could ever concern you by making you an heir to all of God's promises. He is just waiting for you to accept His invitation to enter His rest. *When you work, God rests, but when you rest, God works.* As His power works in you, He is able to bring to pass His purpose in your life and do exceedingly abundantly above your highest prayers, desires, thoughts, hopes, and dreams.

God has a place of rest for you to live every day. He has made it possible for you to live free from worry and fear, simply by trusting in His great love. Believe what He says about you in Christ. Say "Amen!" to His promises! Trust Him completely with your life and just like Joshua and Caleb, you'll live in that place of abundance Jesus has prepared for you. You'll experience the wonderful inheritance you have in Him!

What did you learn today from the children of Israel? How will it affect your life if you refuse to embrace God's opinion of you in Christ?

_____

_____

_____

What did you learn from Joshua and Caleb? How will it affect your life if you agree with the One Who loves you and believe His opinion of you in Jesus?

_____

_____

_____

_____

_____

What did you learn today about God's promise of rest in Jesus, and how will you apply it to your life? How can you live loved and live free?

_____

_____

_____

_____

_____

_____

_____

⁜ Day 3 ⁜

GRACE: THE POWER TO BELIEVE

⁜ Take time to pray before you begin. ⁜

We'll end this week of study by finishing Hebrews chapter 4. Yesterday we read verses 1-13. In these verses, we learned of the promise of rest we have in Jesus. We enter this rest when our hearts believe the truth of who we truly are in Christ.

But our Heavenly Father knew all too well that the enemy would work overtime to convince our hearts of the lie, "You're not who God says you are." He knew we'd be continually tempted to believe this lie, so by His grace He gave us the power to overcome this temptation and believe Him instead.

Read **Hebrews 4:14-16**: *¹⁴Inasmuch as we have a great High Priest Who has [already] ascended and passed through the heavens, Jesus the Son of God, let us hold fast to our confession [of faith in Him]. ¹⁵For we do not have a High Priest Who is unable to understand and sympathize and have a shared feeling with our weaknesses and infirmities and liability to the assaults of temptation, but One Who has been tempted in every respect as we are, yet without sinning. ¹⁶Let us then fearlessly, and confidently and boldly draw near to the throne of grace (the throne of God's unmerited favor to us sinners), that we may receive mercy [for our failures] and find grace to help in good time for every need [appropriate help and well-timed help, coming just when we need it]. AMP*

Read verse 14 again. Now take a moment to remember who you are in Jesus. What is your confession of faith in Him? What have you learned through this study about your new identity in Christ? Finish the sentences below with the truth of who you are in Jesus.

I am the righteousness of God in Christ Jesus, because I am one with Him,

I am _____

I am _____

I am _____

I am _____

I am _____

I am _____

I am _____

I am _____

Have you ever doubted your new identity in Jesus? Have you ever been tempted to believe the devil's lies instead? What does verse 15 tell you about Jesus?

_____

_____

Jesus was tempted just like you and me, to question His identity as the Father's Son. He was tempted in every way that we are, yet He did not give in to the devil's lies. This truth comforts my heart to know that Jesus understands my temptations at times to believe the devil's lies. I have felt weak in faith during moments when my circumstances were screaming, *What God says about you is not true!* Yet, I have found strength to believe my Heavenly Father and rest in His love when I come to His throne of grace.

What promise is found in Hebrews 4:16? Where can you find the strength to trust, when you feel weak in faith?

_____

_____

_____

Even the power to believe is found in keeping our eyes on Jesus. As we turn to Him in our moments of weakness, He will strengthen us with the power to believe who we are in Him.

> **Hebrews 12:1,2** says: *¹Therefore, since we are surrounded by such a huge crowd of witnesses to the life of faith, let us strip off every weight that slows us down, especially the sin that so easily trips us up. And let us run with endurance the race God has set before us. ²We do this by keeping our eyes on Jesus, the champion who initiates and perfects our faith." NLT²*

Hebrews chapter 11 is full of examples of people who chose to believe God in the face of very difficult circumstances. They chose to believe what God said about them, instead of the lies of the enemy. They are the *huge crowd of witnesses to the life of faith* that verse 1 is talking about.

How do we live free from doubt and unbelief and follow their example? How do we live a life of faith, fully trusting our Father's love and believing the truth of who we are in Christ? (Verse 2)

_____

_____

Jesus is the author and finisher of our faith, and He lives in you and me. As we keep our eyes on Him, He creates within us the faith to believe, and He also brings it to perfection. He creates in us the desire and the power to completely trust Him (Philippians 2:13).

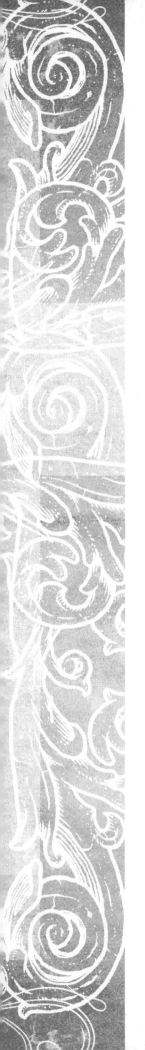

Romans 10:17: *Faith comes from listening to this message of good news — the Good News about Christ.* NLT[1]

Few versions of the Bible translate **Galatians 2:20** exactly as it appears in the original Greek. Paul wrote: *I am crucified with Christ: nevertheless I live; yet not I, but Christ liveth in me: and the life which I now live in the flesh I live **by the faith of the Son of God**, who loved me, and gave himself for me. KJV*

Most translations read, *I live by faith **in** the Son of God.* Yet the power of this verse is found in the truth that we live *by the faith of the Son of God.* We live by the very same faith that Jesus had in His Father's love. Jesus said only what He heard His Father say about Him, and in His moment of weakness He found strength in His Father's love. If Jesus lives in us then we have the same ability to believe the truth as He does. We are one with Him. Paul is saying he doesn't depend on his own faith, but the faith of Jesus, the One Who loved him and gave himself for him.

Your old life ended when it was crucified with Christ. Your old nature, that lived in doubt and unbelief, died with Jesus. That's not who you are anymore. Your new nature is filled with the very faith of Jesus. He empowers you with His faith to believe the Father's love and embrace your true identity in Him.

When you find yourself struggling to believe God, remember that you live not by your own faith, but by the faith of Jesus. He loves you and gave Himself for you so that you could be completely one with Him. In your weakness, He makes you strong!

You lack nothing in Christ! You are complete in Him! You have His ability to trust the Father's love. You don't have to try anymore to have enough faith, simply rest in Jesus. He covered it all for you!

How does knowing that grace is the power to believe help you rest in the Father's love?

_____

_____

_____

_____

What is the main truth you learned today and how will you apply it in your life?

_____

_____

_____

_____

_____

WEEK 10

Eternal Love

DAY 1:
The Greatest Promise of All!

DAY 2:
I Go to Prepare a Place for You

DAY 3:
Death is Swallowed Up in Victory

[17]I pray that Christ will be more and more at home in your hearts as you trust in him. May your roots go down deep into the soil of God's marvelous love. [18]And may you have the power to understand, as all God's people should, how wide, how long, how high, and how deep his love really is. [19]May you experience the love of Christ, though it is so great you will never fully understand it. Then you will be filled with the fullness of life and power that comes from God! [20]Now glory be to God! By His mighty power at work within us, he is able to accomplish infinitely more than we would ever dare to ask or hope. [21]May he be given glory in the church and in Christ Jesus forever and ever"

EPHESIANS 3:17-21 NLT[1]

Day 1

THE GREATEST PROMISE OF ALL!

Take time to pray before you begin.

Learning to live loved by your Heavenly Father is a journey of growing in the understanding of what Jesus really accomplished for you on the cross. The more you receive the truth in your heart the more freedom you will walk in. As you come to know Jesus more intimately, your heart will become more established in the truth of who you truly are in Him and you'll begin enjoying the endless treasures available to you in Jesus. You've learned from Romans 8:39 that the love of God is revealed in each promise you have in Jesus. Every promise is a revelation of His love. As you receive His promises in your heart by agreeing with the One Who loves you, your roots will go down deep into the soil of His marvelous love.

David was a man who grew in the understanding of God's love. The Bible tells us that God himself called David a man after God's own heart (1 Samuel 13:13-14). Listen to how David responded to Jesus in Psalm 23 below. We can see the intimacy he had with God, and that David was living loved at this time in his life. As David renewed his mind to the truth and talked to His Savior about God's promises to him, David's heart was established in God's love.

Read **Psalm 23:** *¹The LORD is my shepherd; I have all that I need. ²He lets me rest in green meadows; he leads me beside peaceful streams. ³He renews my strength. He guides me along right paths, bringing honor to his name ⁴Even when I walk through the darkest valley, I will not be afraid, for you are close beside me. Your rod and your staff protect and comfort me. ⁵You prepare a feast for me in the presence of my enemies. You honor me by anointing my head with oil. My cup overflows with blessings. ⁶Surely your goodness and unfailing love will pursue me all the days of my life, and I will live in the house of the LORD forever. NLT²*

Read back over this Psalm and make it your personal prayer to the Lord. Take a moment to establish your heart in His love. What do these verses reveal about God's love for you?

_____

_____

_____

I love this passage of Scripture; it clearly shows the peace we can live in as we walk this life journey with Jesus. We can live loved by Him, remembering that in Christ we lack nothing! He gives us peace and leads us in paths of righteousness.

No matter what trial we may face, we can live free from fear just like David did, by reminding ourselves of His promises to us. Surely His goodness and unfailing love will pursue us all the days of our lives, and we will live with Him forever!

Read verse 6 again. What promise is found in this verse?

_____

_____

_____

WHEN JESUS DIED AND ROSE AGAIN, HE OVERCAME EVERY TRIAL WE COULD EVER FACE IN THIS LIFE. HE BECAME OUR CONQUERING KING.

In **John 16:33** Jesus said: *I have told you these things, so that in Me you may have [perfect] peace and confidence. In the world you have tribulation and trials and distress and frustration; but be of good cheer [take courage; be confident, certain, undaunted]! For I have overcome the world. [I have deprived it of power to harm you and have conquered it for you.]* AMP

I often think of this verse when I face a difficult situation in my life. It reminds me that Jesus overcame the world for me and deprived sin of its power to harm me. He gave us His great and precious promises so that we could escape this world's corruption and partake of His divine nature (2 Peter 1:4). He speaks His promises to our hearts so that you and I can have perfect peace and confidence in the midst of every negative circumstance we face. In Christ, God has given us so many precious promises for our life here on this earth.

> *The greatest promise of all is spending eternity with Jesus.*

But the greatest promise of all is spending eternity with Jesus. He comforts us by promising that even though we will be faced with trials and temptations in this life, one day we will live free from them all! There will be no more trials, no more temptations, no more distresses, and no more frustrations. Every one of us, as a son or daughter of God will live in the ultimate freedom Jesus paid to give us, through the cross. As Psalm 23:6 says, *I will live in the house of the Lord forever!* Although the average American lifespan is now seventy-eight years, the Bible tells us that our lives here are just a vapor and a wisp. (James 4:14) Eternity, however, will last forever, and Jesus has promised that we will spend it with Him and those we love, in a place beyond anything we could ever imagine.

Surely His goodness and unfailing love will pursue us all the days of our lives and we will dwell with Him forever! Jesus took our sin and judgment upon Himself on the cross so we could share with Him in the riches available to us in Christ. He loves us so much He made each of us an heir of God's blessings here on earth and for all eternity!

Read **Colossians 3:1-2:** *Since you have been raised to a new life with Christ, set your sights on the realities of heaven, where Christ sits at God's right hand in the place of honor and power. Let heaven fill your thoughts. Do not think only about things down here on earth. NLT[1]*

What does your Heavenly Father want you to fill your thoughts with?

_____

_____

In my journey of living loved, my Heavenly Father has given me a glimpse into the place where you and I will spend eternity. My thoughts used to be completely focused on this earth. Lately, however, I find myself longing for the day when I'll see my Savior face-to-face; when all of life's questions and challenges will be gone, and I will finally arrive at the place He has destined for you and me all along. The Bible tells us that we are foreigners in this land (Hebrews 11:8-10) and we are simply passing through this life, heading toward our ultimate destination with Jesus! This earth is not our home; we're on a mission's trip, here to learn to live loved and share God's love with others. We are here to tell of God's amazing grace and to invite others to journey with us to the place Jesus has prepared for those who put their trust in Him.

In this promise of eternity with Him, we once again see the height, and depth of Jesus' great love for us.

Read **2 Corinthians 4:15-18:** *[15]...as God's grace reaches more and more people, there will be great thanksgiving, and God will receive more and more glory. [16]That is why we never give up. Though our bodies are dying, our spirits are being renewed every day. [17]For our present troubles are small and won't last very long. Yet they produce for us a glory that vastly outweighs them and will last forever! [18]So we don't look at the troubles we can see now; rather, we fix our gaze on things that cannot be seen. For the things we see now will soon be gone, but the things we cannot see will last forever. NLT[2]*

What is the result of God's grace reaching more and more people? (Verse 15)

_____

_____

How long will our present troubles last? How long will we experience the glory of God? (Verse 17)

_____

_____

_____

Where do we fix our gaze? Why? (Verse 18)

_____

_____

As more and more people hear about the amazing love and grace of our Savior, there will be great thanksgiving in the hearts of God's children and His glory will shine forth more and more in this world. Our present trials won't last long, but His glory will last forever! So let us fix our eyes on Jesus and all that He has prepared for us. This present world will soon be gone, but He has prepared a place that is more beautiful than any of our eyes have ever seen.

JESUS DIED ON THE CROSS TO GIVE YOU THE PROMISE OF ETERNAL LIFE

If Jesus should tarry, your body will die, but the real you will live forever! He has qualified you by making you righteous so that you can live in the most wonderful place you could ever imagine — spending eternity with Jesus is the greatest promise of all!

Why is spending eternity with Jesus the greatest promise of all? How does that promise reveal His great love for you?

_____

_____

_____

_____

_____

_____

_____

_____

_____

Day 2

I GO TO PREPARE A PLACE FOR YOU

Take time to pray before you begin.

In our last lesson we learned that the greatest promise ever given in Christ is that we who have placed our faith in Him, will never truly die. Even though your earthly body will die, the real you will continue to live for all eternity. Because of His great love, Jesus has prepared an amazing place for you and me to live with Him forever.

> Read **John 14:1-6** *"¹Don't let your hearts be troubled. Trust in God, and trust also in me. ²There is more than enough room in my Father's home. If this were not so, would I have told you that I am going to prepare a place for you?³When everything is ready, I will come and get you, so that you will always be with me where I am. ⁴And you know the way to where I am going." ⁵"No, we don't know, Lord," Thomas said. "We have no idea where you are going, so how can we know the way?" ⁶Jesus told him, "I am the way, the truth, and the life. No one can come to the Father except through me. NLT²*

What did Jesus tell you in verse 1?

_____

_____

What promise did Jesus give you in verses 2-3?

_____

_____

How did Jesus say you could get there?

_____

_____

Jesus has prepared a place for us to be with Him forever. He is the way, the truth and the life. The only way to this place is through trusting Him. **John 3:16** says, *"For God loved the world so much that he gave his one and only Son, so that everyone who believes in him will not perish but have eternal life." NLT²*

What is this place that He has prepared for us like? Let's look in Scripture to discover the most wonderful place your heart can imagine.

Read **Revelation 21:1-7; 10, 11, 21-27:** *¹Then I saw a new heaven and a new earth, for the old heaven and the old earth had disappeared. And the sea was also gone. ²And I saw the holy city, the new Jerusalem, coming down from God out of heaven like a bride beautifully dressed for her husband. ³I heard a loud shout from the throne, saying, "Look, God's home is now among his people! He will live with them, and they will be his people. God himself will be with them. ⁴He will wipe every tear from their eyes, and there will be no more death or sorrow or crying or pain. [For the old world and its evils are gone forever." NLT¹] ⁵And the one sitting on the throne said, "Look, I am making everything new!" And then he said to me, "Write this down, for what I tell you is trustworthy and true." ⁶And he also said, "It is finished! I am the Alpha and the Omega—the Beginning and the End. To all who are thirsty I will give freely from the springs of the water of life. ⁷All who are victorious will inherit all these blessings, and I will be their God, and they will be my children.*

¹⁰So he took me in the Spirit to a great, high mountain, and he showed me the holy city, Jerusalem, descending out of heaven from God. ¹¹It shone with the glory of God and sparkled like a precious stone—like jasper as clear as crystal.

²¹The twelve gates were made of pearls—each gate from a single pearl! And the main street was pure gold, as clear as glass. ²²I saw no temple in the city, for the Lord God Almighty and the Lamb are its temple. ²³And the city has no need of sun or moon, for the glory of God illuminates the city, and the Lamb is its light. ²⁴The nations will walk in its light, and the kings of the world will enter the city in all their glory. ²⁵Its gates will never be closed at the end of day because there is no night there. ²⁶And all the nations will bring their glory and honor into the city. ²⁷Nothing evil will be allowed to enter, nor anyone who practices shameful idolatry and dishonesty—but only those whose names are written in the Lamb's Book of Life. NLT²

What will you never experience again in this place that Jesus has prepared for you? (Verse 4)

_____

_____

_____

Who will inherit these blessings? (Verse 7)

_____

_____

1 John 5:4-5 says: *⁴For whatever is born of God is victorious over the world; and this is the victory that conquers the world, even our faith. ⁵Who is it that is*

victorious over [that conquers] the world but he who believes that Jesus is the Son of God [who adheres to, trusts in, and relies on that fact]? AMP

How does verses 10-11 and 21 describe the beauty and prosperity that is in this glorious place?

_____

_____

_____

What will not be allowed in this place and who will be there? (Verse 27)

_____

_____

In this wonderful place there will be no more crying, and people's hearts will never be hurt or broken again. The people we love will never die and no one will ever be sad or depressed. There will be no more poverty, and no more lack; no more sickness and no more pain. All the trials, challenges, worries, and fears which come at us in this world, will be gone. The old world and everything evil in it will be gone forever!

The Holy City is absolutely beautiful! The glory of God shines in every place. Prosperity is everywhere. Everyone is abundantly prosperous as they walk on streets of gold and live in the most beautiful homes. Everyone will walk in divine health for all eternity! The hearts of God's people will only feel love, joy and peace forever! Nothing evil will be allowed to enter, but only us whose names are written in the Lamb's book of life. What a promise of love our Savior purchased for each one of us!

Read **Revelation 22:1-6, 20, 21:** *¹Then the angel showed me a river with the water of life, clear as crystal, flowing from the throne of God and of the Lamb. ²It flowed down the center of the main street. On each side of the river grew a tree of life, bearing twelve crops of fruit, with a fresh crop each month. The leaves were used for medicine to heal the nations. ³No longer will there be a curse upon anything. For the throne of God and of the Lamb will be there, and his servants will worship him. ⁴And they will see his face, and his name will be written on their foreheads. ⁵And there will be no night there—no need for lamps or sun—for the Lord God will shine on them. And they will reign forever and ever. ⁶Then the angel said to me, "Everything you have heard and seen is trustworthy and true. The Lord God, who inspires his prophets, has sent his angel to tell his servants what will happen soon.*

²⁰He who is the faithful witness to all these things says, "Yes, I am coming soon!" Amen! Come, Lord Jesus! ²¹May the grace of the Lord Jesus be with God's holy people. NLT²

What particularly stood out to you about the place Jesus has prepared for you as you read this passage of Scripture?

_____

_____

_____

What promise was given in verse 3?

_____

_____

In this glorious land there will no longer be a curse on anything. The Bible says the earth we live in now is cursed because of sin. That is why we see mosquitoes, flies and pestilence; why people grow old and everything man builds eventually wears out and needs repair. There are floods, earthquakes, and tornados that bring great death and destruction because of the curse that is on the earth. The Bible tells us that the earth itself is actually groaning for its complete redemption. Jesus is going to create a new heaven and a new earth where nothing grows old or wears out; where everything stays beautiful forever! In fact, a river of life flows through the city and the tree of life will have the most delicious fruit. Jesus promises us that we will reign forever with Him in this most amazing place!

What did Jesus promise in verses 20 and 21?

_____

_____

These are the last two verses of the Bible. Jesus promised, *"Yes, I am coming soon!"* As I read about this glorious place He has prepared for all of us and gain a deeper understanding of His amazing love, I find my heart responding to Him by saying, *"Come Lord Jesus! Come quickly!"*

> Read **Hebrews 9:24-28**: *²⁴For Christ did not enter into a holy place made with human hands, which was only a copy of the true one in heaven. He entered into heaven itself to appear now before God on our behalf. ²⁵And he did not enter heaven to offer himself again and again, like the high priest here on earth who enters the Most Holy Place year after year with the blood of an animal. ²⁶If that had been necessary, Christ would have had to die again and again, ever since the world began. But now, once for all time, he has appeared at the end of the age to remove sin by his own death as a sacrifice. ²⁷And just as each person is destined to die once and after that comes judgment, ²⁸so also Christ died once for all time as a sacrifice to take away the sins of many people. He will come again, not to deal with our sins, but to bring salvation to all who are eagerly waiting for him. NLT²*

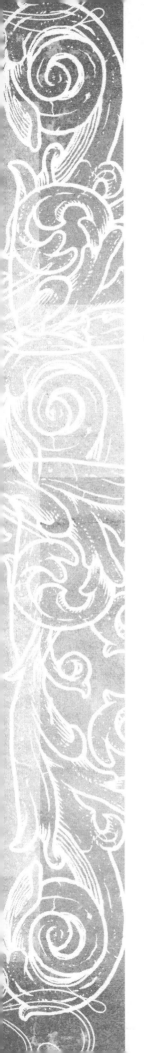

These verses clearly teach that when Jesus comes back, He is not coming to deal with our sins, but to completely save us from the evils of this world. He is coming to bring complete redemption and salvation to those of us who are waiting for Him.

Hebrews 9:28 says, *Christ died once for all time as a sacrifice to take away the sins of many people.* **Hebrews 10:14** says, *For by that one offering he forever made perfect those who are being made holy. NLT²*

You and I have been made perfect forever through Jesus' one sacrifice

When we stand before the judgment seat of Christ, we will be judged righteous in Jesus because of our faith in Him. **Jude 1:24** says, *Now to Him Who is able to keep you without stumbling or slipping or falling, and to present [you] unblemished (blameless and faultless) before the presence of His glory in triumphant joy and exultation [with unspeakable, ecstatic delight]. AMP*

Remember the courtroom scene in Week 5 of our study? When you stand before Him, you will hear Him say with triumphant joy, "My beloved, you are perfect, innocent, justified, and righteous because you placed your faith in My Son Jesus' sacrifice for you. I am fully pleased with you because of your faith in Him."

Let's look at one more passage of Scripture that reveals the wonderful place that Jesus has made ready for us to live in:

Read **Isaiah 11:6-10, 13**: *⁶In that day the wolf and the lamb will live together; the leopard and the goat will be at peace. Calves and yearlings will be safe among lions, and the little child will lead them all. ⁷The cattle will graze among bears. Cubs and calves will lie down together. And lions will eat grass as the livestock do. ⁸Babies will crawl safely among poisonous snakes. Yes, a little child will put its hand in a nest of deadly snakes and pull it out unharmed. ⁹Nothing will hurt or destroy in all my holy mountain. And as the waters fill the sea, so the earth will be filled with people who know the LORD. ¹⁰In that day the heir to David's throne will be a banner of salvation to all the world. The nations will rally to him, for the land where he lives will be a glorious place. NLT¹*

¹³Then at last the jealousy between Israel and Judah will end. They will not fight against each other anymore. NLT¹

What a beautiful picture of perfect peace and love among all people. There will be no more killing or wars; it will be a place of perfect safety. Mothers won't have to worry about their babies; they will be raised in a perfect world, without sin, or harm. This land in which we will live with Jesus forever, will be a glorious place! When I think about this eternal home Jesus has prepared for us, I am once again overwhelmed with His great love. One day we will see Jesus — the One Who loves us completely — and it will be so glorious, and so amazing, and so beyond anything our hearts could ever think, desire, hope, dream or imagine, and we will live with Him there, forever!

What did you learn today about Jesus' great love for you?

_____

_____

_____

_____

_____

_____

_____

_____

_____

What do you love most about this glorious place that He has prepared for you and those you love?

_____

_____

_____

_____

_____

_____

_____

_____

_____

⟨ Day 3 ⟩

DEATH IS SWALLOWED UP IN VICTORY

⟨ Take time to pray before you begin. ⟩

We have spent ten weeks learning to live loved and live free in this world. By living in the Father's love, we can have peace in every situation. We will now end this powerful study by realizing, that in His great love for us, Jesus won us the ultimate victory.

WE WIN BECAUSE OF JESUS!

Read 1 Corinthians 15:42-43, 48, 50-52, 54-57:

> *42 It is the same way for the resurrection of the dead. Our earthly bodies, which die and decay, will be different when they are resurrected, for they will never die. 43 Our bodies now disappoint us, but when they are raised, they will be full of glory. They are weak now, but when they are raised, they will be full of power.*

> *48 Every human being has an earthly body just like Adam's, but our heavenly bodies will be just like Christ's.*

> *50 What I am saying, dear brothers and sisters, is that flesh and blood cannot inherit the Kingdom of God. These perishable bodies of ours are not able to live forever. 51 But let me tell you a wonderful secret God has revealed to us. Not all of us will die, but we will all be transformed. 52 It will happen in a moment, in the blinking of an eye, when the last trumpet is blown. For when the trumpet sounds, the Christians who have died will be raised with transformed bodies. And then we who are living will be transformed so that we will never die.*

> *54 When this happens — when our perishable earthly bodies have been transformed into heavenly bodies that will never die — then at last the Scripture will come true: "Death is swallowed up in victory. 55 O death, where is your victory? O death, where is your sting?" 56 For sin is the sting that results in death, and the law gives sin its power. 57 How we thank God, who gives us victory over sin and death through Jesus Christ our Lord! NLT[1]*

What is the difference between your earthly body and your new heavenly body which you will live in forever? (Verses 42-43, 48)

Your earthly body:

_____

Your heavenly body:

_____

What is God's wonderful secret? (Verses 51-52)

_____

_____

When our dying bodies have been transformed into heavenly bodies what promise will be fulfilled? (Verse 54)

_____

_____

What is the ultimate victory that Jesus has won for you and me? (Verses 55-56)

_____

_____

_____

Death is swallowed up in complete victory. We win because of Jesus. We win no matter what! I remember this one particular instance in my life when I believed God for this person to live and not die, and they died anyway. I was so discouraged about it and felt so defeated. I remember saying, "Lord, it's not fair. I don't understand. It feels like the devil has won." I was feeling perpetual pain in my heart because I was questioning God's faithfulness. I took my heart to Jesus and prayed, "Lord, please show me Your perspective on this. Show me the truth that will set my heart free so I can completely trust You." Then the Holy Spirit led me to read 1 Corinthians chapter fifteen. He then spoke to my heart from these verses, "Connie, you see death as a defeat, but I have swallowed death up in complete victory." It was at this moment, that my perspective began to change. I realized that death cannot defeat us. We win because of Jesus. I began to see this person in heaven: happy, healed, whole, and completely free! I thought, wow, there is no defeat in death. There is complete and total victory!

> **Isaiah 57:1-2** says: _The righteous pass away; the godly often die before their time. No one seems to … understand that God is protecting them from the evil to come. For the godly who die will rest in peace. NLT_ [1]

The Hebrew word for peace in this verse, is _shalom_. According to the Strong's Concordance it means "safe, well, happy; health, prosperity, and peace."

What happens to believers when they die? Why do they experience ultimate victory? (Verse 2)

_____

_____

_____

_____

These Scriptures have given me such peace because I truly understand that the people I love who have died are not dead at all. They are very much alive in Christ. Sickness and death did not win because they are in heaven with Jesus. They are experiencing the glory of God. From now into all eternity, they will experience perfect health and perfect peace! Praise You, Jesus!

Our Heavenly Father has given us victory over sin and death through our Lord Jesus Christ

This understanding has given me a deeper revelation of God's amazing love, and strengthened me to trust Him even more. I don't have to fear disappointment or defeat. Those of us who place our faith in Christ can never be defeated. We can completely trust Jesus to live in divine health as we walk upon this earth, because either way we win! Divine health is our eternal inheritance; purchased by Jesus for us on the cross. We live loved by accepting the truth that by His stripes we are healed! I am constantly renewing my mind to the truth that I am the righteousness of God in Christ Jesus and sickness has no right in my body. Divine health is my inheritance in Christ Jesus. I have chosen to continue believing God's promise to me until I take my last breath, because I know that the real you and the real me are healed and whole in Jesus. Our Heavenly Father has given us the victory over sin and death through our Lord Jesus Christ!

Read **1 Thessalonians 4:13-14**: *¹³And now, dear brothers and sisters, we want you to know what will happen to the believers who have died so you will not grieve like people who have no hope. ¹⁴For since we believe that Jesus died and was raised to life again, we also believe that when Jesus returns, God will bring back with him the believers who have died. NLT²*

We can celebrate the lives of those we love who have died before us, because they are still very much alive with Jesus. They've finished their mission's trip and have gone home to the most glorious place we could ever imagine. And when we finish our mission's trip, we will be with them forever. Although we do grieve when we lose someone we love, we do not grieve like the world because we have hope beyond this life. What a wonderful promise we have in Jesus!

The Apostle Paul, who prayed that we might know the love of Christ and be filled with the fullness of God, said in **Philippians 1:21-25**:

²¹For to me, living means living for Christ, and dying is even better. ²²But if I live, I can do more fruitful work for Christ. So I really don't know which is better. ²³I'm torn between two desires: I long to go and be with Christ, which would be far better for me. ²⁴But for your sakes, it is better that I continue to live. ²⁵Knowing this, I am convinced that I will remain alive so I can continue to help all of you grow and experience the joy of your faith. NLT²

The Apostle Paul, who had once hated Christians, had a revelation of the love of Christ. Although he greatly desired to be with Jesus in eternity, he knew he had not completed his mission's trip here on earth. The great love Paul had experienced compelled him to complete his earthly journey with Jesus, sharing the Good News of God's love and grace with the people around him, to help them grow in their faith.

Perfect Love Casts out all fear of death

Read **Hebrews 2:9-15**: *⁹ What we do see is Jesus, who was given a position "a little lower than the angels"; and because he suffered death for us, he is now "crowned with glory and honor." Yes, by God's grace, Jesus tasted death for everyone. ¹⁰ God, for whom and through whom everything was made, chose to bring many children into glory. And it was only right that he should make Jesus, through his suffering, a perfect leader, fit to bring them into their salvation. ¹¹ So now Jesus and the ones he makes holy have the same Father. That is why Jesus is not ashamed to call them his brothers and sisters. ¹² For he said to God, "I will proclaim your name to my brothers and sisters. I will praise you among your assembled people." ¹³ He also said, "I will put my trust in him," that is, "I and the children God has given me." ¹⁴ Because God's children are human beings—made of flesh and blood—the Son also became flesh and blood. For only as a human being could he die, and only by dying could he break the power of the devil, who had the power of death. ¹⁵ Only in this way could he set free all who have lived their lives as slaves to the fear of dying. NLT²*

What is God's plan for all of us through Jesus? How does each verse reveal His love for you?

Verse 10: _____

Verse 11: _____

Verse 14: _____

Verse 15: _____

Why do you not have to fear death?

_____

_____

Jesus loves us so much that He suffered death for you and me on the cross. Because He did this, He sits next to the Father in heaven crowned with glory and honor. The Father's plan has always been to bring you and me into this same glorious position in Christ, by making us one with Himself. We are His beloved children and we can share the same intimacy with the Father that Jesus does as we live loved by Him. Jesus even freed us from the fear of death. When He tasted death for us, He gave us

the gift of eternal life. We can enjoy our Heavenly Father's blessing upon our lives on the earth, and for all eternity, because of His great love!

Just like the Apostle Paul, we can confidently and boldly say:

> *"I am convinced that nothing can ever separate me from God's love. Neither death nor life, neither angels nor demons, neither my fears for today nor my worries about tomorrow—not even the powers of hell can separate me from God's love. ³⁹ No power in the sky above or in the earth below—indeed, nothing in all creation will ever be able to separate me from the love of God that is revealed in Christ Jesus my Lord." Romans 8:38–39 NLT² (AUTHOR'S PARAPHRASE)*

Why does a Christian who dies experience the ultimate victory that Jesus purchased for them? How does understanding this truth help you trust God's love in a deeper way?

_____

_____

_____

_____

_____

How has learning to live loved and live free, changed your life? Share this Good News with others!

_____

_____

_____

_____

_____

_____

_____

_____

_____

Notes

NOTES

NOTES

NOTES

NOTES

BIBLIOGRAPHY

Holy Bible Special Hebrew-Greek Key Study Edition copyright © 1984 by Spiros Zodhiates and AMG International, Inc.

Merriam Webster's College Dictionary, 10th Edition copyright © 1994 by Merriam-Webster, Inc.

Strong's Exhaustive Concordance of the Bible

Thorndike Barnhart Intermediate Dictionary

We would love to hear how this Bible Study
has impacted your life.

To contact the author, write:

Connie Witter
Because of Jesus Ministries
P.O. Box 3064
Broken Arrow, OK 74013
Contact@becauseofJesus.com

For additional copies of this book go to:

www.becauseofJesus.com

Or call 918-994-6500

ABOUT THE AUTHOR

Connie Witter is a speaker, author, and Bible Study teacher. Her best selling book, *P.S. God Loves You,* has sold over 150,000 copies. She is the founder of *Because of Jesus Ministries* which was established in 2006 and has been teaching Ladies Bible Studies for over 15 years. Her Bible Study, *Because of Jesus,* was published in 2002 and it is the foundation of her life

and ministry. Since 2005, she has held an annual *Because of Jesus Women's Conference* in Tulsa and the outlying areas.

Connie has traveled throughout the United States and Russia, sharing the life-changing message of *Because of Jesus.* She has been the guest speaker at Women's Conferences, ladies retreats, ladies meetings, and has also spoken into the lives of teenage girls. She has also been a guest on several Christian TV programs. Her weekly TV program, *Because of Jesus,* can be seen worldwide through her ministry website, *www.becauseofJesus.com.* Each week she shares the Good News: that we are righteous, valuable, precious, blessed, favored and extravagantly loved by God, because of Jesus. Thousands of lives have been changed through her ministry.

If you are interested in having Connie come speak at your ladies event, you can contact her at Connie@becauseofJesus.com.

Other Books Written by Connie Witter

Because of Jesus Bible Study
P.S. God Loves You
21 Days to Discover Who You Are in Jesus
The Inside Story Teen Devotional
The Inside Story for Girls Devotional

CD/DVD Series by Connie Witter

Because of Jesus
Living Loved, Living Free
Psalm 23

Made in the USA
Lexington, KY
11 May 2018